# The Best Day Of Your Life.

A guide to transforming the
ordinary into the extraordinary.

Jennifer S. White

For more information, contact the author on her website at Http://JenniferSWhite.com

First trade paperback edition July 2014

10 9 8 7 6 5 4 3 2 1

ISBN-10: 1500571741

For Gemma.
Everything I write is for you.

# Table of Contents

# Foreword

Sometimes it seems like common sense is increasingly rare.

In a world where the wealthiest nation with the greatest resources is the least healthy—physically and mentally—and many opt for pills and gimmicks instead of healthy habits, Jennifer's writing is a breath of fresh common sense air. She offers the basics like loving advice from a good friend.

Each day, we are faced with a multitude of decisions, but one of the biggest is the attitude with which we will approach our day. We have the choice to go through the motions and treat life like a giant hamster wheel, or we can approach it with a sense of wonder and gratitude. As Jennifer writes, "Live. Every. Damn. Day. Like. It's. Your. First. (And throw away your bucket list, please.)"

From the basics of beating stress, to more difficult issues like dealing with unwanted change, Jennifer offers up sound advice on having our best life—inside and out.

Whether you are at a turning point in your life, and looking to overhaul your habits, or merely looking to tune up an already healthy life, *The Best Day of Your Life* is for you.

— Kate Bartolotta, author, *Heart Medicine*

# Prologue

Every waking moment that we inhale a new breath and then let it back out is a chance to have the best day of our lives.

This book is a guide filled with tried-and-true practices to help us achieve our highest potential and meet our greatest dreams. The intention is that you sit down with this book and read it in full and then go back and work on specific offerings, one step, one day, one moment at a time.

In first reading, many of these practices will seem simple. It's not until we put them into action that their true challenges become apparent. Yet this is exactly the point: living as our best selves, even on our worst days, is a daily practice and something that requires constant effort and recommitment.

The great news, though, is that if you've picked up this book, you're ready to make that commitment.

So, together, let's begin this journey of raw, mindful, sometimes vulnerable, heart-wide-open living, because, really, is there any other way to find happily ever after?

— Jennifer S. White

# Chapter 1

## Make Every Day Your Best Day

"To stay with a broken heart, with a rumbling stomach, with the feeling of hopelessness and wanting to get revenge—that is the path of true awakening."

— Pema Chodron

There are some mornings when you wake up and you're not really sure how you feel yet—the sky isn't quite dark, but it's also not yet light.

You're awake and ready to move and make coffee, but you're not close to alert or mentally crystal clear.

You had a mixture of strange dreams, compiled of family members' faces you miss and subconscious hopes you didn't even know were there until they so unexpectedly popped up into your night.

You're excited about your afternoon plans and saying good morning to your daughter, but you can't fully explain why you still feel a little mopey and kind of...heart-achy.

And what do you do? When you feel that your day and your mindset could potentially go in several directions? You do this:

You get out of bed—after lying there for a moment.

You let your possibly raw, tender or unexpressed feelings settle into your tissues and your conscious mind so that you're able to be fully present in your life—able to deal with whatever comes up because you're not hiding from yourself or your life—and then you get up. You roll to your side, swing your legs over your bed and you. Get. Up.

You practice yoga.

Ideally, this is a real, physical yoga practice that involves breathing and moving through sun salutes and postures that are designed to release the aforementioned experiences from your tissues, so that you don't carry around yesterday's tensions and burdens. Yet here's the secret: you can practice yoga in many different ways.

Just to name a few: ride a bike, walk on a scenic local trail, chew and taste every bite of your breakfast. Breathe. Inhale. Exhale. Repeat.

You don't let go.

You eventually do—maybe—but you remember for dear life—and you accept that.

I cannot help that I have a memory that hangs onto exact words from a conversation from years ago or the knowledge of exactly the way I felt in a situation, but let me tell you that pretending you don't remember does no good. This is called denial.

Instead, be open to the reality that who you are might not be who you "want" to be. Jealousy, hurt, fear—these are all emotions that are extremely uncomfortable—but it's much worse to pretend that they don't exist.

Learn to acknowledge, accept and name what's going on inside of yourself and your life, even if it's not ideal or welcome.

Hug and kiss.

Hug your children. Kiss your husband good-bye before work. Hug your mother. Kiss your friend on her cheek. Cuddle your dog.

In short, never forget to live the true human experience of touch—we crave it because we need it.

Throw away your bucket list.

Oh, bucket lists; I really don't like these. Why? Because you should already be living every single stinkin' day like it's your first. Will that mean climbing Mount Everest today? Hmmm, probably not since you have a nine o'clock meeting. On the other hand, does this concept shape your every interaction?

Will you kiss your husband good-bye after he irritated you because you never know what the day will bring? Not to be negative, but it's true. This is the real world.

Will you take a chance and ask for that raise you know that you deserve (the proper way, of course) because you've decided to live your life to its fullest every day, and not just on your birthday and Christmas?

Live. Every. Damn. Day. Like. It's. Your. First. (And throw away your bucket list, please.)

Open your heart.

Okay, I don't want to get all syrupy new-agey on you, but this is true: life hurts. It stings in fact. However, if you close and harden and become crotchety and bitter as you age, then you attract these types of people and experiences right back into your life. Open up your heart, even and especially when it hurts.

You got burned in love? Try again. You got fired from your job? Apply for a better one.

The world needs more people who aren't afraid of pain and who know that they are resilient enough to survive, thrive and move on.

Be a phoenix not a lemming.

You are not too old or too young.

Ageism—another one of my arch nemeses. You are not too young to have your own thoughts and ideas and you are not too old to learn new things, to change or to simply love living.

If people around you are telling you otherwise, find empathy for their obviously limited view of their own capabilities and shrug off their words—and then proceed to do whatever the hell you want.

Eat mindfully.

Eating disorders go in many directions. If you are ignoring your body's hunger cues and eating foods that generally make your body feel bad, you are not doing yourself a service as far as pursuing your best day.

So yesterday was a day filled with poor choices? (Or maybe your life up to now has been?) So what. I can tell you from personal experience that our bodies are more regenerative than we often think and that effective change happens when you take baby steps, not running leaps. (You know, the old tortoise and the hare story.)

I look out the window and notice that the sky is definitely a brighter shade of grey. The looming, un-forecasted rain casts a heaviness that I feel in my bones. (Literally, even my once-broken bones feel this weight.) I decide to let the mysterious melancholy that I feel wash over me and through me, rather than turning away from it.

I get up to make my coffee and I look forward to feeling its smooth, velvety texture roll over my tongue.

I breathe and feel my chest expand with air.

I dreamt in black and white last night—I always do. I dream in shades of grey.

This makes me aware that life is a spectrum and not two distinct colors. I want to see each shade for what they are, because that's living my life—that's being authentic and this truth and clarity make each day my best.

I sit with my loneliness and my own inner shades of grey because I know that living from this place allows me to move towards the end of the spectrum that I choose.

I believe that life is a choice.

We can't always choose our circumstances and we might learn to shape and transform our feelings and thoughts through effort, but we still have to own up to our almost primal and instinctual reactions.

So you want to live your best day? Then be you. Feel you. Live every day right where you are.

"To truly laugh, you must be able to take your pain, and play with it!" — Charlie Chaplin

# Chapter 2
## Develop Your Inner Wisdom

If you've never given your intuitive ability much thought, you're missing out.
All of us have an inner guide—but not all of us even recognize that voice anymore. So here are five practical ways to get back in touch with your inner sage.

Build confidence.

Following your inner guidance comes hand in hand with liking yourself. You have to first learn to respect and value your insights—and this isn't that different from valuing yourself as a person. Begin to see the positives in your personality, as well as the happiness that already exists in your life; then let these strengths lead you to be—and live as—a more confident person.

Trust—and follow.

Sometimes my hunches seem silly or irrational. Just yesterday my daughter threw a grape in one direction of our family room, and when I couldn't find it, I finally looked where my third eye had seen it rather than where my other two did—and it was right there, underneath my husband's leather chair, all the way across the room and in the opposite direction of her toss. Sometimes, though, your flashes of insight might not come to such fruition, and that's okay—but learn to give them a shot (puns not intended). For example, are there two ways to drive to your yoga studio and for an inexplicable reason, you strongly want to go only one way? Try it. Who knows, maybe there will end up being some temporary tree trimming, complete with roadblocks on that other route (not speaking from personal experience or anything). Trust your hunches—and then follow them through.

Practice yoga.

Yoga teaches us to connect with ourselves on a deeper level. A consistent yoga practice puts you in tune with your body, your breath, and just maybe, your seat of intuition.

Cleanse your third-eye chakra.

There are several ways to cleanse this chakra, so let me share a few of my favorites. One that's simple and always works, within a range, is to lie down and place a chunk of amethyst or purple fluoride on your forehead, about a finger's width above your eyebrows and in the center. Another is to come into child's pose and feel the press of your forehead on your mat and send calming breath into this area. Yet another is to imagine a deep, rich indigo filling up this entire space, as well as the base of your skull (remember, we all have backbodies—and so do chakras).

Meditate.

I've written so much on meditation techniques—
because there are countless ways to meditate, yet even
the most basic meditations will help you. When you
meditate you get in touch with the real, authentic
you—and it's this same you who provides your
intuition. Additionally, a consistent meditation
practice will teach you to calm down and check in
with yourself without all that mental static getting in
the way.

Try this easy meditation out for starters:
Sit comfortably and begin to scan your body, starting
with your stable base and slowly working your way up
to the crown of your head. As you scan, simply feel the
sensations that arise in your physical body. If you feel
tension, disease or discomfort, then begin imagining a
soothing stream of water washing away these
impurities and strains; leaving behind only relaxation
and suppleness.

We're all born with the ability to follow our gut, but
over time we learn to override our intuition in favor of
our more practiced rational thinking.

This isn't entirely bad. We have brains for a reason,
and life requires a clear, thoughtful consciousness in
order to be successful.

Still, learning to listen to that voice inside of yourself serves you too.

Some of the best moments of my life have come from following the wisdom of my higher self, and some of the worst have come from going against it.
I hope these tips help you begin to tap into the power that lies right beneath the surface of your conscious self; to the power that's intrinsically connected to the "you" that isn't seen with the naked eye.

It's this less tangible you who is special and unique, and I guarantee that this inner self has some insights to share with the rest of you—wisdom that will hopefully make your life easier, healthier and happier.

# Chapter 3

## Don't Let Jerks Bother You

As a writer and as a human being, I receive feedback from others—some of which can feel like a personal assault.

The reality of life is that not everyone out there likes making other people happy. Sadly, there are people who actually derive enjoyment from being nasty to others.

So, here's how you can refuse to not let those jerks upset your equilibrium:

Assess what was said objectively.

If the assault was verbal, then assess if you agree with what was said. Could you take it and use it as constructive criticism even if the delivery was less than ideal? Or was this person's statement to you really only useful as a weapon of hurt (because there was nothing truthful or helpful in it)?

If your honest answer is the former, then try as hard as you can to turn your unpleasant interaction into self-improvement, and if not, then allow your mind to focus on the positive reality of you.

Understand where he/she was coming from.

If the offensive person doesn't deserve to be treated with understanding, you do. Take time to assess the underlying why behind this person's aggression.

Is she jealous of you? Does she feel threatened?

Granted, you can't crawl inside another person's head, so you'll never know for sure where she was coming from, but it will help you to let go of hurtful words.

Learn self-love.

Treating yourself with love is something that should be practiced. Notice, and then focus on, what you like and enjoy about yourself and your life. Go out of your way to not permit negative self statements to live inside your thoughts. There is something real in the idea that thoughts become words and words become actions, so try to force your inner voice to speak with kindness.

With time, it will become your fluent, first language.

Talk to someone who loves you.

Hopefully you have someone in your life who loves you and always makes you feel better. This can be anyone: your partner, your mom, sister, or just a dear friend. Sometimes the easiest way to let go of something hurtful is to unload to another person—and let them say the right things to lift you back up.

Have fun.

Often we just need to clear our energy. Do something you love. Practice yoga and dedicate your mat time to a quality you love about yourself. Watch a silly movie with a friend. Whatever it is, it doesn't matter. Relax and enjoy yourself.

Remember what matters.

Don't give assholes more importance in your life than they deserve. Sometimes the thing that helps me the most is looking at my two-year-old daughter.

Reclaim your own power.

I kind of hate that statement that no one has the ability to make you feel bad without your permission, because people do make us feel bad. Still, there's a deeper truth in this.

In the end, you are the only one who decides to carry around your baggage and to allow other people to affect you. So reclaim your right to your own happiness and to your own personal power. Feel strong in the awareness that, while someone might say things about you, it doesn't make them true—and it doesn't have to be your reality.

Remember, if you meet 500 strangers, there will be 500 different opinions of you, but the only one that matters is yours.

Letting go of hurtful words and interactions with others is challenging—but it is possible.

Most importantly, when we stop carrying around unnecessary baggage, we make room to invite bigger and better things (and people) into our lives—and into ourselves.

# Chapter 4

## Reset a Bad Mood

I consider myself to be a happy person, but sometimes life is just plain uncomfortable.

Part of our life's journey has to involve struggle, and challenging people and circumstances are often excellent catalysts for personal growth. Still, some days just stink.

So here are six easy ways to get out of a bad mood—and back into that happy, joyful person you're meant to be.

Cry.

I strongly dislike crying. My family and I have joked for years that I'm like Lindsay Bluth from Arrested Development. Often, I want to cry and can't find the tears for it. Then, at precisely the wrong moment (like dropping my daughter off at school when a fellow parent and friend asks me a simple, "How are you today?") the tears fall like rain. And you know what? Who cares. Crying is literally a physiological release that's, in part, made to elevate your mood. (Wiki it; it's fascinating.) When you can't fight those tears anymore, don't. Cry. It's okay.

Practice yoga.

It's free and even a mat is optional. Move your body through a flowing series of poses that speak to you, with music or without. You will feel better. When I'm in a funk, I love either a good, sweaty yoga workout or a session of deep hip-releasing postures. As yogis, we believe that we store emotions in our soft tissues, and simply going through these asanas and working out the kinks can by default relieve you of mental stress and tension. If you doubt this, think about how you grip and clench muscles in your abdomen, hips or jaw when you feel upset.

Take a shower.

If you've never tried this, it might sound too easy to work—but it does. The key, however, is to focus on the act of bathing. Let it become a kind of moving meditation, concentrating all of your mental energy on the sensations of washing your skin and hair. From a chakra standpoint, this is extremely cleansing to your root chakra, a chakra that's easily affected by stress and sadness.

Wallow—and then pick yourself up by your bootstraps.

Most of us don't have the luxury of wallowing for too long anyways, because work or child rearing calls us back to reality. Still, we need to allow ourselves the time to feel our unhappiness in order to fully let it go. Embrace your bad mood.

Let yourself wallow—and then force yourself to get back into daily life. Easier said than done, I know, but allowing yourself a brief window of time (a day or two) to sulk is great—as long as you very quickly hop back into your daily requirements. Even if you're still feeling down, the mere act of going through your routine motions will bring you a sense of ease. So have that private pity party—and then fake it 'til you make it. In other words, cry, mope and whine—and then put on a smile, take a shower and get back in the game of life.

Get outside.

Going outdoors is so healing. The lush greens of nature are cleansing to your heart chakra, which can take a big hit during times of depression or sorrow. Clean, fresh air is good for you—body, mind and soul. It's easy to stagnate in a foul mood when we live in the synthetic world we're forced to inhabit. For me, getting in touch with nature helps me get in touch with my self: that calm, still part of me that exists like smooth, glassy water just underneath the occasionally overwhelming currents of life.

Breathe.

When you feel panicked or upset take long, slow, deep breaths. Try this three-part breathing technique, which immediately relieves anxiety.

Think of your lungs as pitchers.

Like a pitcher, you'll "pour" the air into the bottom;
inhaling from your belly (deep into your lungs), up
into your chest and finally into your throat. Also like a
pitcher, you'll pour the air out from the top down;
exhaling out your throat, chest and belly.

Inside of you lives a happy, relaxed soul, but this real
you has to live the life of a human being—with a
person's ups and downs, trials and errors.

In order to get in touch with this joyful, authentic you,
it's necessary to first own your emotions and thoughts.
Pretending you don't feel or think a certain way is
dishonest—and dishonesty doesn't lead to oneness
with your higher inner-self or, for that matter, to
happiness.

Essentially, I'm talking in layman's terms about the
yoga sutra's principle of non-attachment.

Non-attachment doesn't mean that you don't
acknowledge your struggles and your triumphs.
Rather, it's a practice—like all other things worth your
effort—in learning to separate your fleeting external
self (and life) from your internal, eternal one.

When you have a bad day, you know it won't last.

How do you know this?

Because there's a deeper part of you that understands a mood doesn't last forever; that our days are temporary, and likewise that there's an enduring part of you that will survive anything and move on. This part is that authentic you, and this authentic you can get through anything—one breath, one shower at a time.

# Chapter 5

## Beating Stress

We all have stress and strain within our lives. All of us; it's how we choose to deal with them that sets us apart. Here are some easy ways to relieve stress:

Get some zzz's.

I've been sleep deprived since the last month of my pregnancy—and my daughter is over two. Let me tell you from personal experience, life's challenging moments are much harder to deal with when you're tired. Go to bed an hour earlier or steal 15 minutes for a nap if you can. However you manage to get a few more moments of shut eye doesn't matter—just do it.

Get a massage.

I mentioned in my last chapter that yogis and other healers believe that our bodies can hold onto our emotional tensions. A massage not only feels good when you're getting it, it can be beneficial to releasing yourself from long-held stress.

Hug the one you're with.

Hugs are hugely positive for us. Try hugging your partner, mom, sister or anyone you love for two full minutes. You can literally feel the tension drain from your body during a loving embrace.

Yoga Nidra.

Yoga nidra, or yogic sleep, is a science based around our cognitive ability to relieve ourselves of stress. Find a yoga studio near you with a qualified yoga nidra instructor—and give it more than one shot. Often, students fall asleep in the first class (or more); and this relates to many factors such as, ahem, sleep deprivation or your readiness to process the feelings that arise during your yoga nidra practice.

Do something different.

I don't know about you, but I find that life can be stressful when I'm underwhelmed just as much as when I'm overwhelmed. Sometimes having too much time—and too much time to think—is not a good thing. Do something different. Go to your local art museum, visit a friend you haven't seen in awhile, take a trip if you can. Anything—as long as it's different and exciting to you.

Drink water.

Okay, water isn't going to beat all of life's tensions away, but did you know that one of the early signs of dehydration is irritability? Staying hydrated is seriously important to your overall health and well-being. While it might not chase away the blues, it sure can't hurt either.

Eat a balanced diet.

Having a balanced diet is crucial to optimizing your health—and lowering your stress levels. I'm not going to give a nutrition lecture here, but I will say this: eat a diet plentiful in color and not so plentiful in processed foods.

Ask for help.

If you're the kind of person who has a hard time asking for help when you need it, then ask yourself why. People are social creatures. We have families and friends and live in a society because we can't do it alone. Learn to ask for help when you're feeling overwhelmed. Start small. Ask a friend to listen to a concern you have; ask your mother to watch the kids while you take a bath; and by all means, don't turn down a sincere offer of help when you really need it.

Have a physician and see her regularly.

If you find yourself frequently frazzled and anxious, don't suffer in silence. Talk to your doctor. Additionally, make sure you have an annual check-up so that you can catch your health concerns in their early or, ideally, preventable stages.

Life is not always simple and straightforward. We live in a world of complex problems and equally complex answers. Yet, life doesn't have to be hard.

Learning to manage your stress levels is a skill that can be learned, but like all great skills it takes practice. Hopefully these tips help put you ten steps closer to your healthiest, most peaceful self.

# Chapter 6

## When You're Feeling Lonely

Sometimes the world feels lonely.

I remember this feeling striking me as particularly unusual and heavy when my husband and I lived outside of Philadelphia. I was far from my family—yet not as far away as when I had lived in New Mexico—but the crowded city streets seemed to highlight my loneliness rather than alleviate it.

Recently my husband and I relocated again, and it's brought back this sense of not belonging. I think anytime a new and unfamiliar area has to be called "home," it heightens this sense of having too few people to turn to.

Really, in the end, though, only I am responsible for my happiness—and for my feelings of loneliness.

It's not right, for example, that my poor husband gets an unfair share of these feelings when they arise—and I have to be conscious not to depend on him too much. (After all, he is only one person and I am supposed to be a big girl.) So what should we do when we feel alone and there's no easy or obvious solution?

Try a few of these:

Take a bath.

You've got to trust me on this one: taking a bath is a great way to enjoy your alone time rather than wallow in it. Being alone can be luxurious and wonderful (take it from a mom who almost always has to bathe with her toddler these days). Take the time to treat yourself to a nice, long bubble bath (and if you do it my way, make sure there's a plate with dark chocolate and a glass of wine beside your tub).

Take a walk.

Being out in nature is extremely cleansing and uplifting—and it can be a great way to enjoy your solitude. One of my favorite meditations is a walking meditation; where you focus on the sensations of your feet lifting up from and stepping onto the ground. It's very earthy and calming—and a healthy usage of alone time.

Go to a movie.

Yes, I'm one of those weirdos that likes seeing movies alone (not that I don't enjoy company). When I lived in New Mexico, my work schedule was often the exact opposite of my husband's, so I'd pop into that teeny, tiny theater off the plaza and watch a film alone.

I also frequented movies by myself when we lived in Pennsylvania and I traveled with my husband for his job. Give it a shot, or if it's not your style at all, watch a movie on Netflix.

Read.

Reading a great novel is something we generally tend to prefer doing alone anyways. For me, getting lost in a book is one of my favorite passions—and a great thing to do when you're feeling lonely.

Get coffee.

It might seem silly, but one of my favorite places to head during some of our more isolated locales was my small-town coffee shop.

Go to the library.

Libraries, especially these days, are underrated. You just might discover your new favorite book while perusing the shelves, and there's almost always a soft, cozy chair to sit in for a little while.

Branch out.

Do you feel lonely a lot? Think about why. If it's because you're not making friends easily then look for different places where you can meet people with similar values—say, the yoga studio for example.

Get a haircut.

This suggestion might be unexpected, but I have a history of doing things to my hair when I feel lonely or in a rut. It's just hair, it grows back, and you should be having fun with it anyway.

For me, a haircut is such a cathartic experience—and it's almost always invigorating and renewing if you're feeling down.

Become your own best friend.

If you're not already, you should definitely consider becoming your own best friend. For one, life is a lot more fun when you enjoy your own company. Secondly, we tend to meet healthy friends and partners when we like ourselves first; and lastly, it alleviates a lot of feelings of loneliness if you like being with yourself.

I've always needed alone time, but my first big, adult move out West with my husband was surprisingly enlightening.

I learned a lot of things about myself by being forced to spend more time alone than I would have previously chosen to do. These tips and suggestions are things that have really helped me throughout the years when I felt isolated and alone—and I hope they help you if you're in a similar place in your own life right now.

Remember, though, that life should be a social, fun experience, so if you're feeling lonely a lot, don't ignore it. Talk to someone you trust.

Having said that, I love The Verve song "On Your Own" that says "you come in on your own and you leave on your own." It's a reminder that we're supposed to experience moments of solitude; we are solitary—and that doesn't have to be a bad thing.

# Chapter 7

## The Little Things in Life

I can't explain the way a really wonderful song makes me feel.

Alive. Inspired. Sad.

I literally get goose bumps from a powerful tune that touches me.

I can't explain the way I feel when my daughter smiles at me.

Alive. In love. Soulful.

There are some things in life that touch me deeply, on a level where words typically fail.

These are the things that make life worth living.

Still, life is the daily motions of plugging along and getting through each minute.

Standing in line. Being somewhere when you'd rather be somewhere else. Having too much on your plate.

Yet when I stop and really think about what it is I'm rushing around for—where my impatience with the actual, physical process of living my life stems from—I never have a good enough reason.

Then I think about the moments in my life when I've been truly happy. Again, happy or touched on a level that's difficult to even convey. These moments are small.

Sure, my wedding day is up there, and the birth of my daughter was miraculous, of course; but it's the tiny things that happen while I'm waiting in line—like the sincere smile my daughter gave the cashier when she handed her a sticker. These moments are the root of my internal feeling of satisfaction.

So what am I rushing for? What am I rushing to? Death? The next line?

Why do I want to be somewhere else?

Example: I'm participating in a teacher training right now and finding it extremely challenging to be apart from my toddler.

The thing is though, I've been dying to take this training, and I deserve to enjoy it—and my daughter deserves a mother who stays in the present moment because otherwise I'd miss the kiss she gives me when she's sitting on my lap and I'm reading *Mr. Brown Can Moo!* to her for the hundredth time; I'd miss that if I was ignoring her and making a "necessary" phone call instead.

Remember that every single time you wish a less-than-perfect life moment away you're by default wishing away those other "nothing" moments that make up your meaningful existence. Those sweet smiles and connections—they happen on an infinitesimally small scale too.

Life can give us goose bumps, and it can give us headaches, and I don't know about you, but I wouldn't want it any other way.

# Chapter 8

## On Making Friends

Making friends is so awkward—but so enlightening.

I haven't moved around that much in comparison to others. I grew up in a small northwestern Ohio town and then moved to a nearby college town to attend university after my high school graduation.

In the middle of my Bachelor's degree I followed my boyfriend (and high school sweetheart—and now husband) out West for his first Master's degree. Then we moved back East for his first professional job, and then we moved back to Ohio for my hubby's second Master's, and now I'm in a new part of the Buckeye State for an awesome job in his new field. Phew! I guess I have moved around a bit.

If you're wondering where I'm going with this, I've been thinking lately about how these relocations have affected my ability to form friendships—and stay true to myself.

Every time you make a new friend you are confronted with the reality of wanting to hide parts of yourself while letting the aspects of yourself that you love shine brightly.

Whether or not we outwardly admit it, we're constantly confronted with the pieces of ourselves that we don't really like every time we make a new friend.

Conversely, I'm reminded of my favorite hobbies, interests and general self-qualities that I enjoy because new faces and conversations draw this out of me or remind me of them. It's a truly fascinating self-study to see how you react when you meet someone new.

Are you overly self-involved when you speak? Do you ask so many questions that the other person feels bombarded? Do you pretend to be someone you're not just to fit in? Are you unnecessarily frank and honest when the situation doesn't call for it? Or are you Goldilocks seeking what's just right?

The ironic thing is that when we turn on our listening ears and genuinely interact with another person, we can learn not only about other people and the world, but we can learn an awful lot about ourselves—our goals, characteristics, indulgences and fantasies.

So in honor of love and friendship, here are a few things to consider when meeting new pals:

Smile.

The world needs more smiles.

Whether or not it seems like you're always new in town, smiling at other human beings is one sure-fire way to attract other positive people.

Stay open.

Sometimes life hurts and isn't fair—but if you close yourself off, you will not meet the people that will help your life radiate joy and happiness.

Be honest.

Sincerely, please don't say that you like to play tennis because you met someone cool who freaks out over the game, while you've never even picked up a racket. If you really like this person and want to stay in touch, the truth will come out, and if you don't, then who are you trying to impress?

Live a little.

Life should be fun, and new friendships are great opportunities to do something different and to shake it up. Go dancing with a new friend or hit the nail salon to talk and be pampered simultaneously. Don't be afraid to have a little innocent fun.

Ask your spouse.

Assuming here that you have a supportive spouse, your partner's opinion on your friends can be very insightful.

Often having an outsider's perspective with an insider's concern is a great way to make sure you're meeting additional supportive people for your life.

Enjoy your alone time.

This might seem counter-intuitive for a chapter on friendship, but I fully believe that loving yourself helps you seek out healthy partnerships.

Practice yoga.

Sorry, I had to throw this one in there. If you practice yoga, you'll get this. Having such an important value in common is a great way to begin a friendship.

Be vulnerable.

I was recently with two new, yet very adored, friends, and I found myself sharing things that I almost wished later that I hadn't; but you know what? People that you love deserve to know you completely—so that they can love you back.

Be open.

Some of my most valued friendships have come from following my own inner dreams (like my yoga training when I met my dear friend Jane). Following your passions leads you to other similarly passionate people—even if that wasn't your original intention. It's like a bonus or an unexpected gift.

Making friends is not easy, period.

We're forced to confront our own egos, ugliness and authenticity—which is exactly what makes these experiences so valuable.

So the next time you find yourself in a situation that requires you to extend yourself out to others, consider these suggestions, and remember that life is a social event—and maybe it's time to send out a few invites.

# Chapter 9

## Becoming Your Own Hero

I can be an extremely "heady" person.

I often get stuck in my thoughts and inside of my mind and, I swear, it almost feels at times like I've forgotten that I even have a body.

And there's nothing wrong with being this way—a lot of creative people are like this too.

On the other hand, we are physical, primitive beings, just like any other animal on God's green earth and we need to remember this, if only to continue to be able to create.

For example, the concept for the book I'm working on right now came to me while (gasp!) living my life.

So here are ways to get back in touch with the rest of ourselves, especially when we've gotten stuck within our brains—so that we can once again be the real-life heroes of our stories:

Practice yoga.

This one cannot come as a gigantic shock.

The physical practice of asana is specifically designed to move energy within our body and release physical blockages.

This isn't all hooey and hocus pocus, either—tension is stored inside muscle tissues; areas we clench and tighten when experience mental or emotional frustration—and taking these tissues through a range of yoga postures helps us to create a body that's supple and strong—and more prepared for the next challenges that will surely arise.

Get outside.

I was walking with my dad the other week and I told him that I think a period of melancholy I had been going through was directly attributed to being trapped indoors.

I have a toddler and live in a chilly winter climate and it's just not possible for us to head outside for our one to two-hour daily walks, like we'd become accustomed to before the cold weather hit.

Nature is where we are meant to spend time. We are not created to be cooped up in cubicles on computers all day. And, although this might be somewhat unavoidable, just getting outside for five to ten minutes is both refreshing and invigorating to us—body, mind and spirit.

Have sex.

Sorry, Mom.

Yet, this is true.

If you're a consenting, safe-playing adult, making love is one of the best prescriptions for getting out of a mental rut and back into the clarity of a happy body.

Cheat on your yoga mat.

Yes, yoga class is amazing—but it's not the only thing out there that can help to heal your body and heart.

Sometimes taking a spin on my circa-1980s Nordic Track is a surefire way to make me feel blissed out and ready to take on life again.

Throw away your limitations.

Yes, I'm a cerebral sort of lady—but if I tell myself, and others, that I am something, I'm limiting myself.

I'm boxing myself into a self-constructed category of who and what I am—and what I'm capable of.

So, guess what else I tell myself I am?

Here's a laundry list: an athlete, an all-around do-gooder, a hard-worker, and, last but not least, someone who's capable of anything.

If you find yourself feeling pressured to live or behave in a certain manner, then consider trying, for one day, putting on a new label that you admire but think you cannot wear. (My guess is that you'll be surprised—and that this new name tag might never come off).

Because, the thing is this, life is only what we make it.

And, what are we waiting for (I mean, really)?

The only thing I'm waiting for is to see what next hurdle my mentally creative mind wants to help me hop over.

# Chapter 10

## The Brilliant Clarity of Life's Beauty

The snowy scene outside my large, front picture window, the one that takes up my entire living room wall, reminds me of a postcard.

Bright white cotton slowly and steadily blankets my driveway and builds up on the thick line of evergreen trees that lies between my nearly private street and myself, as the early-morning sun glows a soft orange from in between the tree branches, peeking out as if to say "Good morning."

I look out at this quiet, picturesque backdrop and I feel the vulnerable rawness of my unusually rough past few days melt away ironically as the icy precipitation continues to grow and swirl.

It fascinates me that when life's fragility strikes and haunts me, that this beauty that's obviously always surrounding me becomes sharper and clearer around the edges, like a picture in perfect focus; yet it's more delicate too, and almost painful to behold.

I find that I'm impatient to others' criticisms and lack of politeness (perhaps rudeness is too extreme for me to claim in my overly sensitive state).

But I'm definitely too fragile myself to spend any time arguing these points.

Instead, I concede and don't feel defeated or weak for doing so; I actually feel a strange calmness and strength in my bending-near-breaking state.

My toddler parades around the wood floor of the living room in her florescent elephant footie pajamas singing "Twinkle Twinkle Little Star" perfectly on key. She's recently discovered that she can perfectly pronounce "up above the world" so she sings this refrain over and over. Her melodic voice fills the room along with the light from the rising sun.

I look again out our big, front picture window. The snow has quieted so much that it almost appears to have stopped falling. Likewise my emotions are gentler now, streaming through me more evenly, and I look out and notice that this blanket of snow has become littered with patches of sunny glimmer.

"What glitters isn't always gold," I hear whispered softly in my ear.

I have to remember to hold this fragile beauty when the darkness is gone and the world is less scary and ruthless. I have to remember why the snow falls too heavily at times, more thickly than I'd like or feel I can even handle.

"Up above the world," my daughter sings, pointing with her tiny finger out the front window at this bright yet curiously fuzzier, more unclear representation of the same dramatically stark, crystalline landscape I've been so wholly immersed in.

I try to mentally imprint on my self for later that these snowstorms happen so that life's real beauty can show, more apparent when all the rest—this disingenuity of the happy ruse—is shadowed over.

# Chapter 11

## Dealing with Anger

I have a truly scary temper.

By nature, I'm an extremely fiery person. One of my all-time favorite movie quotes is Babe the Pig saying that he might be small but he's "ferocious when provoked." I've stolen this statement and used it many times (although usually when I'm feeling playful rather than stormy).

I'll be the first to admit that I have a long road ahead when it comes to releasing and properly dealing with my anger, but I'd still like to share with you the tips I've learned thus far. Here are things to do (and not do) when you find yourself in a rage.

Don't blame others.

While other people can surely incite emotions in you, you alone are responsible for your actions. Period.

Walk away.

Give yourself a time out before you actually need one. I've read that Buddhists believe you should learn to walk away when you're angry. I don't know much about Buddhism, but I can attest to the benefits of learning to do this.

Whether you get angry just about every day (ahem, I'm sheepishly bowing my head now) or you get p.o.'d once a year, you know that you're getting angry before you explode and say regrettable things. Learn to have enough self-control to walk away and wait out your anger.

Say "I'm sorry."

If you find yourself unable to walk away, or unable to walk away in time, then by all means say I'm sorry. Yes, the actual words; and for the love of God don't say "I'm sorry, but." The only butt in the room is you, end of story.

Acknowledge who you are.

I consider myself to be passionate in general, not just temperamental and prone to anger. I'm only in my 30s and I don't believe in saying never, but I will say I consider it highly likely that I'll always be easily excitable; although that doesn't necessarily mean that I can't learn to control it. (However, if you know any old people, you'll understand what I'm implying when I say that my temper will still likely come back to haunt me full force in my advanced years, since the elderly seem to always be overly honest versions of their true characters. Hopefully it'll be cute in a Sophia Petrillo sort of way by then.)

Anger is a secondary emotion.

This is not a psychological principle. It's my opinion. (I only took Psych 101 and that was at 8am during the beginning of my freshman year. I don't remember doing well.) Still, anger is not what you truly feel. Of course, you're pissed, but really, underneath it and if you dig deeply enough, you'll absolutely find another emotion like fear, hurt or regret (even before you actually say something you wish you could take back). Get in touch with this primary emotion and, not only will your anger fade more quickly, you'll be doing yourself a big service by delving into this real you— and your real emotions.

Laugh at yourself.

Taking yourself less seriously will benefit you in multiple ways—including your temper tantrums. Sometimes the sulky elephant in the room is your own ego.

If you find it difficult to let go of your ego in relation with your short fuse, then think about how ridiculous you look when you're mad. (Go ahead and picture Donald Duck. Yeah, you look even dumber than that.)

Lay off me, I'm starving.

Before you allow yourself to act from a place of anger, assess whether or not you feel irritable because of a physical rather than emotional or intellectual reason.

(Remember: being irritable is one of the early signs of dehydration!) Make sure you're taking care of your physical needs too.

Having vulnerability is not the name of a contagious disease.

This is kind of a culmination of several of these tips, but I believe that being angry is deeply connected to not being able to show, or even experience, vulnerability. Get over it.

Life is hard enough. Learning to not make it harder on yourself is a huge step in the direction of healthy— and happy—living. Remember that we're all human and we all have good and bad qualities. In fact, I don't think it's an exaggeration to say that all of us get angry at least from time to time.

So give yourself a break when you slip up, but get back on the horse and keep on trying. Controlling your anger (or better yet, getting rid of it entirely) is respectful to the people around you—and to yourself.

## Chapter 12

## Recipe for a Successful Life

"My recipe for life is not being afraid of myself, afraid of what I think or of my opinions." — Eartha Kitt

I just got off the phone with my sister.

She witnessed a terrible injustice today in her job as a social worker.

I look over at my daughter—so small, fragile and dependent upon protection despite her sassy, can-do attitude—and I'm struck square in the chest with the forceful realization that these types of injustices occur daily and hourly and over and over again.

And I might not be able to help (Lord knows my sister tries). I might not even be able to keep my own child safe (although not for lack of effort and perseverance), and this sickens me.

Yet, as I glance towards her curly hair and soft, peach-pink skin and large, intelligent, kind eyes, I see *my* success as a human being—in her tiny person, my whole life is given more meaning than every "A" that I earned in college or every mile that I pushed myself through when I ran or any amount of success that my writing will bring me.

Because the most important thing in a recipe for success is two-fold.

Initially, we need more than goals. We need hopes and dreams and sandcastles in the sky to build foundations underneath—and then we have to be open to the flowing, swirling, mutable way that life unfolds despite our best laid groundwork.

My own hopes and dreams have a fundamentally unchanged core, but much of what I want changes as I give myself permission to grow and shift and, in short, become wiser.

So, for me, my starter recipe for success looks something like this (you know, like a starter for bread dough...I digress):

A well-rounded cup of imagination.

We are at our best when we are inquisitive and capable of understanding that there is more to unearth than what we've been given to work with.

Several dashes of humor.

Maintaining a sense of humor gives us the confident foundation to stay malleable enough to go with life's twists and turns—and fun is absolutely part of the successful journey.

Copious amounts of self-love.

Yes, love in general is grand, but true love begins with loving ourselves.

If it's been a long time since you've treated yourself with love, then take the baby step of having a gentler inner voice (the way that you would speak to a young child or a beloved friend).

A handful of fire.

I'm a nice person. Sincerely, I am. However, my recipe calls also for the ability to stand firmly and tenaciously when I need to in my own convictions.

A pinch of cynicism.

Because it's okay to insist on looking outside of the box and it's more than okay to question and stay curious.

A shake or two of money.

We need money to live. As a chakra enthusiast, I often keep within the back pocket of my mind that my spiritual self is nurtured and nourished by an equally practical self that wants to care for my basic human needs.

(You know, that whole *a tree has roots* thing.)

A hunk of willing to get dirty.

And I don't mean playing dirty or anything undesirable.

But we do need to remember that if we want to hang out in sandcastles in the clouds, then someone has to get a little messy building that foundation.

A couple smidgens of forgiveness.

Successful people will fall. More, they expect to fall and to fail.

It's wonderful to have the aforementioned fire and tenacity to get back up, but it's even better to forgive yourself for not living up to expectations.

One thing that I find helpful is to recognize that my falls are teaching tools and learning experiences towards my larger success rather than simple, unnecessary set-backs and obstacles.

And your recipe might ask for varying amounts of these ingredients, but that's the best part about being a master chef—you can create your own new, brilliant—and previously unknown—recipes.

"As a single footstep will not make a path on the earth, so a single thought will not make a pathway in the mind. To make a deep physical path, we walk again and again. To make a deep mental path, we must think over and over the kind of thoughts we wish to dominate our lives." —Henry David Thoreau

# Chapter 13

## Happy Self-Reflection

Self-growth can mean focusing on your beauty rather than your beast.

I've been feeling compelled lately to examine my own flaws, which isn't new for me. What is new, however, is how I treat these subsequent discoveries.

As I roll through my life, I'm confronted constantly with my own positive and negative qualities.

I'm confronted with my selfishness, my aggressiveness, my ego, my woundedness—in short, my inner torments. Yet, I'm also confronted with my positive attributes: my passion, compassion, strength and fragility.

In the past, I've spent countless hours trying to improve these "lesser" personality traits, but my new approach is to examine these personal attributes and shrug my shoulders with a "huh, that's interesting" and then move forward, pursuing how I can positively affect the world rather than focusing on this negativity.

The reason behind this revolution of optimism is simple: focusing on the negative, even if it's to correct yourself for the better, is putting your energy in a bad place.

This doesn't mean that I still don't want to improve. It means I think these self-adjustments will happen more gracefully, more effectively, and possibly even more rapidly, if I concentrate my energy on the good.

At the same time, I don't mean to suggest that I, or anyone for that matter, am only made up of black and white, good and bad, evil and heavenly. I learned a long time ago that to be idealistic is to be black and white, and the world is made up of shades of grey and reality—and this reality is that I have a long way to go in some areas of my self.

Still, I've come a long way in other areas. I definitely think I've made some real inner triumphs that have paid off big in how I ultimately treat other people and what I offer to society as a whole, which has encouraged me to ponder, why do we not give ourselves enough credit?

Why do we more often than not insist on beating ourselves up over our failings? Why are we so negative about ourselves?

I guarantee there are people out there that don't focus on making themselves better people; that just focus on having fun.

I have to speak honestly and say that I don't relate to these people at all, and while I certainly pass no judgment (and if I do it's envy), this chapter is not for these types.

This chapter is for the people who, like me, fight their own demons every single day while sadly ignoring to give their angels a pat on the back.

Yesterday, I dropped my daughter off at school 15 minutes early because I needed some space for myself to breathe before I walked into my teacher training, but instead of feeling rejuvenated, I berated myself over my action and ended up walking into my classroom feeling lower than low. I felt like a terrible mama, all because I dropped my little lady off a few minutes early. Wow, was this an eye opener for me when I really stopped to think about how much it affected my attitude.

I'd like to share with you a little check-list of things to give yourself encouragement over, especially if you're like me and prone to harping on your less-than-heroic ways.

- If you try every single day to put your best foot forward, despite or in spite of what personal trials you're in the midst of, then give yourself not only a break, but a well-deserved congratulations.

- If you smile at others in order to share a little bit of happiness with the world (especially if it's a smile in the direction of someone who challenges you), then give yourself a smile in return.

- If you wake up every single morning and get out of bed, even when the day, at first glance, is dark and gloomy, then let your own need to survive and push ahead shed some light into your world.

- If you love with an open heart even though you know that to be so open means to also be open to hurt, then love yourself too.

- Last but not least, if you insist on committing to daily efforts at self-improvement, then make sure to acknowledge that other 99 percent of you that needs no changing, no altering; commit to realizing that you are indeed already perfect the way you are.

The reality for me, as I've already shared, is that I'm a very "heady" person.

I often get stuck in my thoughts, in my brain, and in this false world that I create for myself—and this leads to expectations that ultimately end up deterring me from being my best self.

I've come to the conclusion during my most recent self-studies that for years I've failed at improving the most damning parts of my personality—and apparently it's time for a new approach.

I long to be as selfless as my husband.

I yearn to be more present with my daughter. I crave the ability to stand tall in my confidence while radiating my humility. It seems I've reached a fork in the road of getting to these spaces. So instead of taking the arduously and notoriously long road of bitter self-belittlement, I'm following my bliss and carving a new path to my enlightenment.

If you happen to pass me on this easier but more direct route, be sure to stop and say "hi."

# Chapter 14

## The Plateau to Enlightenment

Sometimes the road to self-betterment stalls, and you're left with a slightly uneasy feeling.

I've always been the sort of person who tries to improve myself.

I put effort into practicing both kindness and honesty.

I've spent a long time working on my natural inclinations towards worry and being quick to anger (and my subsequently sharp tongue).

The thing is, sometimes we just are the way that we are—and that's when we need to work on acceptance.

Because we can't always change everything about ourselves, even when we desperately want to and even when we desperately try.

Trust me when I say that I'm much more patient now than I used to be, though I'm still the kind of person who easily jumps to both conclusions and action, and that there are also moments when these qualities have worked for me.

Because that's another thing: more often than not our personality traits can be viewed as a coin with two sides.

———

One is generally more positive, socially acceptable and internally easier to welcome, and the other is rougher, coarser and, perhaps, less desirable to either ourselves or to those around us.

Today, for example, I felt ho-hum.

You know, one of those grey days where the sky drips a few tears and so does my ceaselessly imperfect heart.

I try so hard to be the person who I know that I truly am, and I still feel that I come up short—quite a bit short, actually.

And on these types of days, the world isn't my oyster. It isn't my playground or my jovial stage to share jokes and make my friends and family laugh.

It's a cold and harsh place that I'm forced to inhabit and then unwillingly call home and I feel like I fit nowhere.

So on days like these, when my fragile chest feels like it's filled with pointy grains of sand that serve no better purpose than to weigh me down, and my mind has a few too many cobwebs, I can't help but wonder why on those other more positive and profound days I care so much about making myself a better person in the first place.

Still, I can't help it.

There's something in the core of my being that honestly believes we're here to learn, to think and to grow, both from our experiences and from our obstacles.

After all, life's challenges are often what force us to evolve, and to become better—it's these days where the sun stays behind clouds that usually offer hidden lessons, and hidden spots of sunshine that wind up peeking out eventually anyways.

And I guess I'm not even sure if most people are like this.

I've definitely met people who don't appear to be working an awful lot on their social consciences, much less making their way down the path of more a meaningful, and less tangible, growth (call it enlightenment if you want).

And at the same time, on gloomier days, I'm reminded that sometimes self-betterment and self-growth resemble more of a plateau than a world-record mountain climbing expedition—because we need to include acceptance and love for the people who we are in this moment, right now, along with our efforts of improvement.

If we don't give ourselves permission to make mistakes while still maintaining a sense of tenderness, then how can we possibly extend that kindness and love that we're seeking back out into the world?

I think it's true that you need to love yourself before you can fully love another.

So, unfortunately, my little temper might be larger than I'd like it to be, and my patience might wear thin a tiny bit too easily for my satisfaction, but I'm also passionate and hard-working—it's the flip-side of that coin.

And I like me.

I like who I am, even on days like today when I'm sitting in my bed writing with a face that's a touch too serious and stoic.

I like myself enough to remember that stopping to smell the roses is part of this road that I'm on—the one that leads to my higher self—because if we don't periodically pause and enjoy the view, then we're missing much more of the point than we realize.

"Knowing others is wisdom, knowing yourself is enlightenment." — Lao Tzu

# Chapter 15

## Be More Beautiful (Almost) Instantly

Beauty is not only skin deep; beauty radiates from the inside out.

Don't believe me? Think of the people that you're drawn to or find attractive, and likely there's something beyond physical beauty drawing you in.

Charisma, happiness and a warm personality absolutely help boost physical attractiveness. So here are five ways to feel more beautiful—and look more beautiful—(almost) instantly.

Exercise.

Exercise has physical benefits for your body that show up and help you shine. Working out helps your skin— and inner light—glow (thank all those mood-boosting chemicals). It also helps with weight management and improves self-esteem. Sounds like a good beauty fix to me.

Smile.

This one is instant. Your heart lightens and it shows on the outside the second you turn up the corners of your lips. Give it a try.

Cleanse from the inside.

I'm reading a wonderful book about the Yamas and Niyamas in my yoga training. One of the important beauty-related lessons here is that our society is obsessed with outer cleanliness and sadly pays little attention to what's going into our bodies to keep us clean and pure. Pay attention not only to what you eat and drink but to what you read and who you listen to—and then pay close attention to what you're saying to others in return. There's a deep inner peace that comes from living a life of cleanliness—and I'm not talking about stocking up on expensive skin care products.

Dress well.

I know it probably seems shallow to move from the last tip to this one, but it's true no matter how you want to count it. Dressing well helps you look and, more importantly, feel better. I remember my twin telling me in high school that on days I was feeling less than stellar I shouldn't throw on a baggy old t-shirt, I should put on my favorite, form-fitting dress and rock it—and she was absolutely right.

Confidence.

Wow, this one's extremely hard to tell you how to accomplish. Still, if you're confident in yourself (and in more than just your outer appearance), it will show and it will make you more attractive.

Again, think of someone you find attractive. I guarantee that physical perfection isn't part of it, because none of us is perfect. Yet, these quirks, these individual little traits that make you you, actually make you more endearing.

Step one in boosting confidence (let's start one step at a time): stop saying nasty things to yourself. Trust me on this one. Like I've said, thoughts become words and words become actions. Talk to yourself the way that you would a child—with patience, kindness and love. Developing this sort of soft inner voice will help your outer voice resonate more beautifully—and your outer appearance too.

Don't get frustrated if you wake up and roll out of bed, and don't feel at the top of your game. We all have down days. Instead look in the mirror and focus on what you love. Spending time focusing on the positive reinforces these attributes and helps them radiate out into the world. You are beautiful.

Give yourself permission to share your beauty with the world today and every day.

# Chapter 16

## The Power of Positive Thinking

I taught a yoga class for the first time in almost a year yesterday.

I've been teaching yoga for about five years, but ever since my most recent move my regular teaching and private sessions have been non-existent.

There are several reasons for this, but the main reason is that my family is now too far away to watch my small daughter while I'm away (and, quite frankly, one of the reasons I built a career around a flexible—no pun intended—job is so that I could be home with my little girl). I'm on several area sub lists, but even those opportunities often don't coincide with when I have help.

Still, despite my years of teaching, I'm participating in a yoga teacher training and one of our requirements is co-teaching a class at the studio. Initially I was overjoyed. Then I started to over think it, like I do everything else.

I practiced more for this class than I have for any other class in my career thus far, including workshops.

Don't get me wrong,

I've always gone to class with a plan, but part of my adoration of Vinyasa yoga is the ability to go with the flow (again, no pun intended).

I'm an anal type-A personality, and my mat (and my teaching time) is the time to tune in with my intuitive side; to tune into the energy of the students and of the room; to create a session that goes with this energy rather than against it, even if that means going against an original class plan.

As a teacher, this happens frequently. You walk in with something in mind (possibly a super cool power pose you're freaking out to show your regular gang), and then everyone's overly subdued and low key when you arrive—and you have several newbies who have never practiced yoga before. You change up your flow routine, and class rocks anyways.

However, after a year left hanging out in the pen waiting for the gate to open, I began to feel so excited that my nerves kicked in. I doubted not only my ability to teach, but sadly my desire to teach. Wow, what a dark place to be in as someone who thought for years that I've been one of those lucky people who lives my passion through work.

Then it hit me—I was giving my confidence and my positive outlook away.

At first I was angry with myself.

I realized, though, that staying angry and upset only served to fuel this terribly negative fire, when what I needed was to totally transform my view—and I needed to get back in touch with my optimism. Thankfully the time leading up to this actual class date allowed me the opportunity to put these realizations into practice.

My twin sister (and former, regular yoga student) came in from out of town for the class. I turned my thoughts around by looking at this upcoming weekend as my long-awaited chance to visit with her instead of looking at it as my nerve-racking date of teaching for the first time in a year. (My co-teacher was even more anxious because it would be her first time teaching live ever.)

The morning of class, I wouldn't let anything negative into my brain—or out of my mouth.

My sister tried to talk to me about an upsetting dream she'd had overnight, and I said, "No! Stop! I can't listen to anything bad before I teach."

I didn't check my email in the hours leading right up to our start time either.

I got to the studio and saw my visibly cheerful, but scared, co-teacher, and I wouldn't let her say anything negative or nerve-related—and you know what, my positive thinking worked.

Sure, we both put a lot of time into coordinating a kick-asana yoga routine (pun intended). Yeah, we have personalities that gel. Alright, she worked her butt off practicing her cueing skills since it was her first time teaching a real class. Yet neither of us missed a beat or messed up one pose—and I still believe there's something deeper than even hard work or luck.

It's the power of your positive mind—your positive thoughts; your positive words. They all add up. They all matter.

Every word we speak or think adds something to the world around us—or takes something valuable away. So if you want to live in a bright, sunny place filled with love then stop thinking and verbalizing hate.

Stand up for your beliefs, and stand up for your right and your ability to make a change in our world—one word, one thought at a time.

# Chapter 17

## Stop Being Afraid of Happiness

Are we afraid of happiness?

I can look back at points within my life and remember thinking that this moment, right now, is so good that what comes next must surely be bad.

Even when this proved true, I was still doing myself a disservice by thinking this way, because I wasn't allowing myself to fully enjoy the happiness of that moment. Instead, there was something sad and strangely...synthetic about it.

I don't consider myself to be a masochist, but this surely can be considered self-punishing behavior.

Are we afraid of happiness? Why do we think happiness is something fleeting, temporary and delusional? Is it because we don't want to be happy or because we don't know what to do once we are?

It seems that much of our life is spent trying to "fix." We try to fix others; we try to fix ourselves; we try to fix everything and anything in order to feel safe and secure in the real delusion that we can control our situations in ways that are actually very much out of our realm of control.

Does happiness actually bother us because it can't be controlled?

There's something passionate and surreal in a true moment of contentment. We feel attached to another person, if the moment involves a spouse or a friend, in a way that can be unnerving if we spend too much time thinking about how intrinsically connected we all are.

In other words, finding happiness with another individual, my husband for example, means that my happiness is in some way dependent upon him, and for many of us such a dependency is frightening, and it goes against our often independent ways of thinking.

On the other hand, there's the simple reality that underlying the most joyful, optimistic thought patterns lies a very negative mind.

In short, even if we try to view the world positively we can't help thinking that because we feel good this means that our next life experience surely must be bad because life isn't, and can't be, all good; and, yes, there's obviously merit to this way of thinking, but it serves to foster fear, anxiety and, basically, anything but happiness.

So what can we do to stop being afraid of happiness?

We can mindfully stay present with our current happiness by breathing, and reminding ourselves that it's okay to be happy, and that we deserve it.

We can remind ourselves that we don't need the continual drama in life that being a "fixer" brings. We can experience life and not like how some people behave or how some things turn out for us, but that doesn't mean we always need to step in and fix it.

We can practice yoga, because yoga allows us to embrace the sensations present in our bodies and our minds; and it allows us to reflect on how the simple things in life, like breath and movement, really do equal happiness.

We can mindfully stay present when life is uncomfortable. Not checking out when things get ugly encourages us to fully embrace the present moment, and this serves to connect us with the beauty that always resides there simultaneously, even when it appears hidden.

We can acknowledge that being happy sometimes triggers our pessimistic thinking.

So much of life is spent setting and accomplishing goals. John Lennon once said that "Life is what happens to you while you're busy making other plans," and this is so true.

If we spend our life imaging what could have or should have been, we're by default not enjoying the happiness of where we ended up.

Happiness is scary because it means that we might fall—and it's true we might—but if we live life waiting to fall down, we're always falling.

Life ebbs and flows. Happiness ebbs and flows—and that's okay. It's okay because the converse of all of this is also true.

When we're living shadowed beneath the darkest cloud, we know that soon it's the sun's turn to peek back out and fill our world with light—and happiness.

# Chapter 18

## Listen to Your Gut Instinct.

I was getting ready this morning to take my little girl to her music class when I heard the plunk, plunk of freezing rain.

I was not excited.

My husband had to leave early for a morning meeting and I asked him to start our car. I was trying to throw myself together quickly after our bath. (I just about always start my day by sharing a bath with my little lady; I highly recommend this over a second cup of coffee for enthusiastic energy.) Anyway, I was trying to hurry so as not to leave the car running for too long.

I noticed how heavy the freezing rain had become as we headed out the front door, and the back of my shoe caught on the corner of the door. This has never happened.

My instant reaction was this is a sign to stay home.

Instead, I got in my car and backed out of our garage. I already felt the slip and slide of my tires as I rolled down my driveway.

Afraid, I stopped the car, and my shoe catching on the front door sprung to my mind's eye.

I pulled back into the garage and walked back inside, with my confused toddler in tow.

We can make up her music class on Wednesday morning. What's the point of risking injury when my gut is flashing neon lights of warning?

It got me thinking about all the times throughout my day—much less my life—when my internal instinct is trying to tell me something and I either listen or I ignore it. You know, those small things during our days that end up making up our lives.

Here's a list of occasions I came up with when it's important (but not always easy) to listen to your gut.

Shut your yapper.

There are times when I want to speak sharply or caustically in the fit of the moment and my inner guide says, "Stop!" Unfortunately, I can think of several times I wish I had listened.

The road less traveled.

There are absolutely moments when my inner driver has steered me down a different route to my destination (literally while driving).

The occasions when I haven't listened and instead gone my usual way haven't, so far, brought me major distress.

However, often I get stuck behind a garbage truck or the road is down to one lane as a tree-cutting crew works along the power lines—and I almost always wish I'd listened to myself because there was really no negative reason not to.

Your child.

My daughter is the reason I began listening strongly to my instincts again. Something is telling you not to walk away for that split second to grab your coffee from the next room, and you wish you'd adhered to your own advice when she trips and falls. Just a hypothetical example, of course. There are also other times when I've listened to my internal mother's intuition—which began on day one—and I'm so thankful. Especially if you're thrown into an experience with someone such as a physician, who can sadly be an intellectual bully, you might be less inclined to trust your own parental voice. Make sure you remember that no one has a better "degree" in your child's behavior than you.

Don't buy that.

This might sound frivolous, but how many times has your voice of wisdom suggested you not purchase that handbag or pair of shoes and you bought it anyway—then that item sat in your closet unworn and unloved. What a waste of money—and what a waste of a great chance to listen to your intuition.

Don't eat that.

Your inner voice is a great wellness coach. My instinct very rarely encourages me to eat two extra cookies or have a third glass of wine. Just sayin.'

Talk to her.

Another instance when intuition frequently becomes obvious to me is when I meet someone that I know, on a deeper level, I could be friends with. I then have the choice to either say "Hi" and begin a conversation—or not.

Do this not that.

For me, this usually relates to my child. I might feel like looking at so-and-so's Facebook pictures for a couple more minutes, but then I look over at my little girl, who's climbed down off of my lap and is now handing me a book to read. My instinct doesn't tend to say, "Jennifer, go ahead and ignore your daughter and click on that photo." Still, how many of us are guilty of putting the people in our lives on the sidelines for significantly less important things?

Stop it!

For me this relates to my temper (and also relates to the first suggestion). I'll begin to get angry when my better self says, "Halt! Leave the room for awhile!" Oh man, are there sooooo many times I wish I'd listen. I try extremely hard to now.

Try it!

—

That book club at your yoga studio or that cool class a friend invited you to attend: things that are on your wish-list of desired experiences that you put on the back-burner for no real reason. This came up a couple weekends ago when I was invited to dinner and an inspirational movie with fellow yoga instructors. I desperately wanted to go, but I knew that it would be a challenge for my family if I was gone a second night that week. When I mentioned it to my hubby, though, he was actually annoyed that I had considered saying no. Life is too short to constantly say "No" to things that we really want to experience, especially if these experiences are healthy and enriching.

Get out of that job.

Many of us are stuck in positions out of pure necessity. We have families and houses and bills to pay—all of us.

Yet, a few years ago, when my husband toyed around with getting a second Master's degree in order to switch to a field, and a job, that had been calling his name for years, I said, "Full steam ahead!" Why? Because surely additional student loans and all of the stressful aspects of returning to student life were concrete reasons to turn his opportunity down, but thinking of all the years that he has left in the work force was the only reason I needed to encourage him to say yes. Say "Yes" to bettering your life, even when it's hard—especially if your inner voice is behind it.

Ultimately, there are many times throughout our daily life when we have distinctly clear opportunities to head down one path or another, and often, if we listen, there's a (granted sometimes almost inaudible) voice inside that's trying to help us know exactly what to do. What I'm suggesting is that you begin to listen and take note of the consequences.

God gave us brains for a reason, and we certainly need to listen to our intelligent rational reasoning, but much of life isn't easily defined into "this is good" or "this is bad." We have a few great options, and all of them have benefits and disadvantages—and these constantly presented circumstances are the ones that ask us if we have the guts to listen to our gut.

Maybe you need to hone your listening skills. I know I do.

Give it a shot and see what unfolds for you in your life.

I'll end this chapter with a quote by one of our best-known thinkers (who happens to be a lesser known proponent for listening to your intuition), Albert Einstein.

"The intuitive mind is a sacred gift and the rational mind is a faithful servant. We have created a society that honors the servant and has forgotten the gift."

# Chapter 19

## Little Ways to Live Our Best Lives

Those annoying, little chores in life that we avoid or procrastinate about are just as important as seeking enlightenment.

Don't get me wrong, I happen to firmly believe that working on your inner rock star is crucial to how well you live your life. Self-betterment is something that we all should be working on and towards. At the same time, though, life is those seemingly minor moments when we're asked to do something that we don't want to; those "little" things that we should do if we truly want to live our lives as our best selves.

Things like...

Exercise.

You don't like to exercise? Who cares, do it anyway. Just a short walk around your block a few times makes you a healthier person—and the cool thing is that if you push through not wanting to do it, you might arrive at that unexpected place of enjoyment when you do.

Say "I'm sorry."

You have a hard time saying the words "I'm sorry." Well, news flash, so do a lot of people who still say it. Offering the chance for forgiveness to someone else is incredibly self-serving actually, and, unfortunately, we all occasionally act in ways that merit an apology from time to time—and you might be surprised at how much better you feel afterwards.

Eat vegetables.

This might come as a shock, but our taste buds crave what we eat. Meaning, you might have to force down those green spoonfuls a few times before you actually begin to like them.

Stop bending your elbow.

In college, one of my favorite teachers was my nutrition teacher. He was a big, well-dressed man with a rich Southern accent. He constantly dramatically mimed eating in front of the class, and said we have to find the willpower to stop bending the elbow (i.e. quit putting more food in your mouth). As a recovered anorexic, I am more than fully aware how intrinsically food can be connected with emotions. However, the reality is that what we eat— and don't eat—affects the quality of our lives. Putting this into practice does take willpower, but I know you can do it.

Smile.

If you work with someone who challenges you, then, congratulations, you should meet every other person on earth who experiences this too. Smiling at someone who knows how to push your buttons is a skill that should be practiced every day.

Clean up.

This will probably be something I have to practice for the rest of my life. I strongly dislike cleaning (as do many people), but everyone loves the feeling of living in a fresh, inviting space of health and cleanliness. This means that I have to pick up my dust rag and get to it, even when I don't really feel like it. (Bonus, cleaning is good for your root chakra.)

Live by example.

Something that everything on this list could go for is the importance of teaching your children through example. I remember a fellow college student, who was also a mother, telling me that she wished her children would eat vegetables like I did. I, in turn, asked her if she ate a wide variety of veggies herself. She replied no, that she didn't like them. Well, how interesting then that your children won't eat them either. We absolutely cannot ask or demand our kids do one thing while we blatantly disregard our own advice.

Say "I don't know."

Pretending to know the answer to every question that comes your way is bogus, whether you're a college professor or a stay-at-home yogi like I am. None of us have all the answers, so quit pretending to be a know-it-all, because it makes those times when you do have something worthwhile to share significantly less special.

Share the how.

People are too often told what we should be doing rather than being told how. In other words, it's so easy to tell someone to do "good" or to "let it go," but how often do you share how you let it go? A lot of the "sage" advice out there is junk.

I don't want to hear one more person tell me to love my enemy. However, I'll gladly welcome more thoughts on how you're going about doing that in your own life and experience.

There are so many things I could add to this list, and I'm sure you feel the same way. Still, you have to start somewhere.

While I plan on continuing my path to yogic enlightenment, I have to be honest about that fact that I'm living a human existence with human responsibilities, some of which might seem unimportant or minor.

Nothing in life is minor. It all adds up.

—

Taking out the trash without complaining means that my husband didn't have to do it this morning when he didn't have time. That's living kindness with someone important in my life; that's a concrete way to show my affection—and sometimes showing love and living your journey towards enlightenment means changing out your laundry instead of changing the world.

So excuse me, I have to get running. I think I hear a recycling truck.

# Chapter 20

## Letting Things Go.

Being a writer is great practice for learning to let things go in life.

I'm frequently bombarded with difficult and sometimes what feels like unfair criticism—much like life.

Recall that if you meet 500 people, you'll hear 500 opinions of you. This is so true. Let us consider momentarily that we take into account these opinions rather than completely discarding them.

One of those reasons is that, sure, it's often best and healthiest to let terrible feedback about yourself go. However, listening to others can be beneficial if you don't let it hinder or deter you from your journey towards happiness.

Additionally, if how we are perceived by others didn't matter so much, then it wouldn't be so hard to let go of painful critiques in the first place.

So here are a few ideas on how to let uncomfortable words or experiences go.

Think about the other person's perspective.

Yes, you can't go inside someone else's head, and yes, you shouldn't waste much time (if any) trying. Still, trying to understand where another person was coming from helps to not take things personally (which inspires attachment). Example: I came home from class and was excited to share a thought with my husband who wasn't appearing very receptive. When I asked him about this, he said he simply wasn't feeling well, but he did want to hear what I had to say (and he added to stop internalizing so much). Okay, lesson learned.

Feel it.

I think one of the worst things we can do (or one of the best, if you want to have a hard time letting go of stale emotions), is to not feel what we're really feeling. I tend to get angry, and I can easily hold onto that anger for longer than I even want to admit if I don't get in touch with the underlying feeling behind that anger (because, in my humble opinion, anger is always a secondary emotion). Allow yourself to feel what you are really feeling—pain, hurt, grief, etc.—so that you can face these emotions and then release them more naturally.

Do something else.

For me, I get easily stuck in my head—very monkey mind-ish. Often the thing I need to do the most in order to let something go mentally (like a thought that just keeps revolving around, polluting my thoughts and making my inner self a toxic environment) is to do something else. I know it sounds too easy, but it actually works. Exercise, watch a movie that you can really get into, or (my favorite) get outside. Like I've said, nature itself is very cleansing. Change your scenery to facilitate change within your thought patterns.

Admit you need help.

Having said that, anyone who's moved a lot knows that your burdens and baggage come along for any ride. If your issue is something stronger than a little mental obsession you need to let go of, then you definitely need to own that and deal with your dilemma. If it's a constant, reoccurring problem like tension with a prominent family member or trauma from a past event, then seek professional help.

There's nothing wrong with asking for help, especially if you feel stuck in a rut you can't seem to move out of.

Write.

So you're not quite ready to open up to someone in a professional setting, and your friends are sick of hearing you talk about your problems over and over again (especially if it's the same problem).

Journal writing (or blogging, if you really adore writing) can be very cathartic. Writing out your thoughts and feelings can help connect you with new ideas and ways of looking at something that you don't fully recognize until you're working through it on paper (or computer).

Five ways to work through seemingly overwhelming problems can seem like an underwhelming number of solutions, but when really practiced and sincerely delved into, these suggestions all take time, practice and patience. In other words, if they seem too easy to work, then you haven't tried them yet.

## Chapter 21

## When You're in a Funk

I'm not sure why, but sometimes "the funk" knows how to find me.

You know, those days that feel blah and cold and grey—and the sunny, gorgeous outdoor weather is certainly not to blame.

I haven't written in almost a week, which for me is seriously crazy. I write (or think about or wish I was writing) daily. Why haven't I? Because I've been in a funk!

Yet, great things happened to me these last few days, don't you doubt. Regardless, the funk knows no logic.

Of course, I've always been moody, but the interesting thing about those grey days is that they happen to everyone. Everyone. I don't care how happy, cheerful, positive or generally well-versed in your yoga practice you are—an occasionally "eh" day will find you.

So what can the ordinarily grateful person do to get out of the funkiness?

This stuff:

Remember tomorrow.

Yes, I'm that nerd who belted out "Tomorrow" like I was orphan Annie reincarnated. I love this song, and I love its message. There is always, absolutely tomorrow.

Look at the bright side.

Annoying when you're in a bad mood, yes—but checking out that sunnier side of life is purposeful. Focusing on those awesome, amazing little moments that lifted your spirits will help lift them back up—even just the touch you need when your mood sours .

Play with a child

My two-and-a-half year-old daughter teaches me so much about life—and bad mood busting is no exception. Small children don't hang on to words that hurt or things that happened yesterday. Take a page from that book.

Lighten up!

All too often my bad moods are caused by placing too much seriousness on myself, my life, or the world in general. Lighten up and learn to laugh at yourself.

How? In my experience, if I'm really needing to manage my overly self-centered nature, the universe has a way of doing it for me—like a bird in a tree pooping on my head at just the right (or wrong) moment.

If you aren't lucky enough to experience this type of divine reoccurring behavior, then be your own reality check by remembering to laugh at yourself when you fall rather than cry or scream.

I think I could go on and on here because, as I alluded to earlier, I'm perhaps blessed with regular foul funks. However, I tend to look at them now as an excellent opportunity to practice my mindful awareness of the "now" moment, and as chances to remember my yin and yang, light and dark way of thinking.

We're given these times in life to dwell on—or be haunted by—dismal experiences and moments, because they only serve to highlight the blissful, truly peace-giving ones that happen next.

So keep your chin up, keep practicing yoga, and if that doesn't work then Google good ol' orphan Annie and shout at the top of your lungs that "the sun'll come out tomorrow."

# Chapter 22

## On Being Human

"Find a beautiful piece of art. If you fall in love with Van Gogh or Matisse or John Oliver Killens, or if you fall love with the music of Coltrane, the music of Aretha Franklin, or the music of Chopin—find some beautiful art and admire it, and realize that that was created by human beings just like you, no more human, no less." — Maya Angelou

There's something wonderful about being human.

We can stroll down city streets, taking in interesting people and the tallest of buildings.

We can move through nature; feeling the crunch, crunch, crunch of gravel beneath worn tennis shoes, gazing up between tree branches at blue sky.

We can cuddle up to those we love under soft blankets, cradling our infants and lovers while looking into their eyes to see their souls.

But sometimes being human isn't a sensuous experience or a sharing of love.

No, sometimes it's comparison and discomfort and loneliness and abandonment—because being human has a wide meaning and vast connotations.

But it's hard to not fit in.

I spent much of my life trying to be like everyone else and then a nice chunk of my teenage years pretending I didn't give a damn what anyone thought (even to myself). It's taken years to strike a balance between being satisfied with my own approval as enough and being honest with my needs for love and respect from others.

Still, on a random day when the sky isn't so blue and being human feels slightly like a large burden, I'm thrown from this fine-tuned equilibrium by a seemingly minor hurt or similar wounding human act.

And on any such random day, I'm my own enemy; I am my own layer of injustice.

I keep myself in a quaint but cozy box of self-construction; its paper-thin walls my own self-perception and its contents what I envision myself to be in that particular moment of my life.

This changes, though—I change.

I change as I allow myself to either burn my self-imagined cage or as I push out one wall, perhaps even incorrectly thinking it only a temporary investigation of what lies outside.

And change itself feels like this.

Advancement is slowly toying with new ideas, new people, new jobs and new places; it's experimenting with a different flavor of life—whether by force or desire—and realizing that our palate has much broader taste then we knew.

Yet we can disappoint ourselves.

We say sharp words to someone we love, more than any other human.

We become anxious in a situation that calls for calm clarity.

In short, we feel challenged by an aspect of life and then, in our human minds, we fail.

But failure, too, is a significant part of the human condition.

Success and failure, however, are not polar opposites. Rather, they are brothers and sisters on a greater quest: a quest to be human.

And to be human is to seek out love and work and shelter, along with hope and possibility. To be human is to understand both being a supremely rational creature and an insanely irrational animal too. We're this compelling mixture of emotion, materialism, philosopher and scholar—each and every one of us, our own unique blend.

So, how do we practice being human?

We open our eyes to our own splendor.

We open our eyes to the magnificence of those around us.

And we open our hearts to the tender, gory reality that our perceived flaws and failings are, in their own less obvious ways, also brilliant.

"I try to avoid looking forward or backward, and try to keep looking upward." — Charlotte Bronte

And when falls are unavoidable—when the ground is suddenly beneath our disjointed noses—we consider how our trips, our lapses and our exposed defects are, ironically, the same traits that make us decidedly more beautiful.

# Chapter 23

## Everyday Practices

Many worthwhile things in life really do take hard work and practice.

Here are some daily practices that will serve to make your life healthier and happier:

Mindful eating.

When you're about to pop something into your mouth, ask yourself if you're doing so because you're hungry, or if it's for another reason. There's nothing wrong with eating something just because it's good or because you're socializing, but food is meant to be fuel for your body—and practicing eating with awareness will serve you physically, as well as mentally and emotionally.

Positive thinking.

If you frequently catch yourself being a Debbie Downer, then spend more time practicing being conscious of your thought patterns. There really is an underlying truth to the concept that thoughts become words and words become actions, so speak your words more carefully—and positively—if you want to have a more optimistic outtake on life.

Giving.

Giving from a place of love and joy within yourself brings joy and love back into your own life. Practice giving without any intention of receiving, and you'll likely find you have more to give than you thought possible—and more space to receive life's happiness in return.

Yoga.

As one of my teachers said to me this weekend, practicing yoga is practicing connecting what you're thinking with what you're doing. If you're driving your car, you're thinking about driving your car. Trust me, all of us need to practice this. Why? Because we'll get more fulfillment out of what we're doing, and because there's so much joy in the little things that we miss when we let our minds wander.

Listening.

Listening is another thing we all need to practice—and I'm not just talking about waiting for the other person to finish speaking so that you can say something. Nearly all of us are also guilty of trying to fix others or trying to offer advice. Practice listening to someone else and try to refrain from speaking in return. Often all we really want is to say something out loud to someone else, not to be told what to do.

Breathing.

Okay, I know we do this on our own quite naturally and without practice, but practicing breath work will benefit your body and mind by bringing yourself into yoga, and focused, deep, steady breath is intensely calming to you physiologically.

Saying no.

Practice using your voice, so that it matches your heart. If you find yourself often saying "yes" to a commitment that doesn't serve you or really isn't even possible for you to do (and then bowing out of this commitment later), then say "no" the first time around. Think about why you want to say "yes." Ask yourself what you're afraid of. Usually we're afraid of disappointing others or afraid of rejection, but you're letting yourself down if you spread yourself too thin.

Saying yes.

Conversely, how many times has a new friend asked you to go to lunch, for example, and you said "no" when you could. Possibly you wanted to, but again encountered fear (fear of not having enough to say; fear of not having enough in common; fear, fear, fear). When life hands you opportunities that are healthy for you and healthy for your life, are you saying "no?" Say "yes" instead.

Turning off technology.

I'm by no means saying to stop emailing, using Facebook or reading the news. I am, however, suggesting that instead of flipping on the TV or your laptop when you're bored that you, I don't know, go outside or read a book. You know, things that have existed for many, many years that you stopped doing because your iPhone is handy.

Self-love.

How do you love yourself? You begin by speaking kindly to yourself. Has your inner voice become quite harsh? Would you speak to a friend or a stranger the way that you speak to yourself? I truly believe that the first step towards loving and accepting yourself is to talk to yourself the way that you would a child—lovingly, kindly and patiently.

Many of these practices might seem easy in thought, but give them a shot, every single stinkin' day, and see just how difficult—and rewarding—they can be.

So go ahead, turn off your computer or phone and then commit to doing any, or all, of these practices—starting today.

# Chapter 24

## Fake it 'til You Make It

I've often been viewed as a confident sort of gal, when my reality is that my natural tendency is to be insecure.

Yet I learned to fake confidence early on—and there's one main reason why.

Ever heard of "fake it 'til you make it?"

Keep in mind that I'm a yoga teacher and a writer with a degree in geology. In other words, I'm not writing this for a psychiatric journal. (Although, I do hold a minor in sociology—that sound you heard was a button flying off my shirt, hitting my wood floor, as I puffed up my chest to help give this some extra merit.) Still, faking it 'til you make it works, never you fear.

It works when you're sad. You know, when you watch your favorite hilarious movie—the one you've memorized all the lines to—and you end up feeling better.

It works when you're feeling withdrawn. You go to that socially obligated get-together, put on a smile and extend your hand to your friend's friend, and you leave the party feeling more like a happy social butterfly than a lonesome recluse.

In other words, in life, we sometimes have to do things because we don't have a choice. Duty calls and we answer, because we're grown ups—and part of being a grown up is dropping residual childhood insecurity.

Here are a few ways to (temporarily) fake confidence:

Stand tall.

I can still hear my dad telling me as an awkward pre-teen to stand up straight with my shoulders back. He never said it to me like he was a military drill sergeant either, he said it with love, because he wanted me to feel good about myself and to project that out to others. First of all, having good posture is an instant confidence booster—and it really does help display your self-worth. Try imagining that your sternum is connected to an imaginary string, and that as this string is pulled up, your heart lifts and your shoulder-blades naturally slide down your back and relax. Also, lift up from the crown of your head while softening through your jaw.

Smile.

People who smile win people over, plain and simple. I see it already with my toddler, who's an innate flirt. More importantly, smiling helps you feel and then send out happiness into our world—and what's an easier self-esteem fix than that?

Make eye-contact.

A recently discovered pet peeve of mine is lack of eye contact. It's like some people have no awareness that you should look at the other person during conversations and when you, say, smile at them.

Notice how it makes you feel when people make eye-contact with you, as well as how it makes you feel when they don't. I honestly think that a quiet smile, emanating from your eyes and then radiating down to your lips, is more effective than a bunch of fancy schmancy words—and I also think that making eye-contact shows self-confidence.

Quit apologizing.

Okay, I'm the first person to suggest learning how to say "I'm sorry." For some, it takes work to learn how to make an apology even when it's desperately needed, while others say "I'm sorry" way too easily. On the one hand, when you do need to apologize for real, it will mean significantly less, and on the other, you're giving away your own value every time you apologize unnecessarily.

Laugh at yourself, not others.

One thing I've learned from being a writer is that our senses of humor vary considerably.

Since I'm positive that I'm hilarious, I'll let you in on a little secret—it's much funnier to be able to laugh at yourself than to try make a joke at someone else's expense. (Which, in my not-so-humble opinion, actually stems from a lack of self-esteem.)

Say "thank you."

When you're offered a compliment say "thank you." That's it. Thank you. Don't add in that this silly little skirt only cost you twelve dollars or that you don't think so but...(voice trails off into self-deprecating comment of choice). Why? Because it's not necessary. Take the compliment, and consider that it's true. The end.

Look in the mirror and see your value.

Do you look in the mirror and see only the things that you don't like? Well, stop it! Start paying attention to the attributes you love about yourself, because that's what other people see when they look at you. For one full day, try looking in the mirror and noticing all the things you love about yourself (or better yet, don't look in the mirror much at all).

Dress well.

My sister told me when we were teenagers that I should always wear my best dress on the days I felt the worst about myself, and was she ever right.

Dress the part. If you're feeling frumpy, then wearing frumpy clothes will only serve to foster this feeling. Instead, dress to impress (yourself).

Surround yourself with love.

Surrounding yourself with people who think highly of you encourages your own self-appreciation. Make sure that the people you invite into your life, and into your heart, deserve to be there.

Fake it, but only 'til you make it.

Flaunting phony self-esteem for too long will wind up falling flat if you don't back it up eventually. If you struggle with severe confidence issues, then try talking to someone (possibly professionally). Sure, I'm advocating initiating your search for self-confidence with a little jump-start, but I'm not encouraging you to be unauthentic. After all, learning to get in touch with the confidence that you already possess—that's buried beneath the garbage that we all collect as human beings—is really what I'm trying to get you to do.

We're all stars. We all shine brightly—and it's these different lenses that we're shining through that color our world with beauty.

Use these tips to re-connect with your own inner rock star, rather than present a falsely contrived picture of someone else's ideal of what you should be—because when we connect with our true inner value, we stop needing the approval and authorization of others anyway.

So get out there and show the world what you're made of.

"Don't be satisfied with stories, how things have gone for others. Unfold your own myth." — Rumi

# Chapter 25

## Getting Lost Can Help Us Find Ourselves

Your weakness is your strength.

I woke up this morning with eyes practically swollen shut from all the crying I had done the night before, when I had gone through the oddest experience.

I've moved around a little bit in my life, but this is the first place that my husband and I really have ever planned on setting down roots.

We have a toddler, and are close to our families, even if it doesn't feel close enough more often than not.

He has a good, stable job that he loves, and the area has great schools for our little one and great hiking and biking trails for all of us—what more could a girl ask for?

For it to feel like home, I realized last night.

I was driving to a meeting for a new yoga studio that I plan on teaching at weekly. (It'll be my first regular teaching gig since our relocation here about a year ago.) Anyways, I knew where I was going—ish—or at least I thought I did.

My GPS took me to the middle of a parking lot in a defunct, abandoned shopping center, and declared that I was indeed at my desired destination of Panera. Huh?

I called my friend, this new studio's owner, and she told me to plug in Target, which I had known was in the same plaza. Of course, Target (with an address very close to where I was supposedly already at) magically appeared. I hit "go" and told her I would be, unfortunately, late.

I proceeded to blindly follow my GPS device, trusting to end up someplace not in the middle of a practical cornfield, and wound up back on the highway. After many twists and turns and exists to other highways, my GPS again declared me—now totally and utterly lost, mind you—at Target.

I was in the ghetto at a Church's chicken.

Yes, I am a writer and, no, I don't have a smart phone. Ironically, I'd been missing the good ol' days recently—you know, the days when you pulled out your ginormous Rand McNally map and figured out your own way, nothing digital required.

Long story made at least a little bit shorter (because there is significantly much more to my unwanted, adventurous tale), I found my way home.

I missed our first staff meeting and I was crying so hard while I was driving that I had to focus even more on my fluid, calming breathing patterns because I had begun to have trouble seeing the road.

I walked in my front door, having kept in touch with my beautiful parents who were visiting for the day in order to watch my daughter, while I had dressed up and put on make-up (I even put on eyeliner) and left for a rare night out. (Hey, I know it's a meeting at Panera, but I do not go out much. Okay, at all.)

My dad told me after comforting me that "If you want to get lost, follow someone."

Isn't that the truth.

I had put so much faith into a piece of technological machinery that I couldn't even tell you if I'd turned right, left, south or north. I couldn't even find my way back to where I'd come from, as if I knew where that was anyway.

The thing is, I don't cry.

However, I always say to beware of what you have to verbalize that you are or you aren't. If you have to state it, then maybe you're actually questioning it.

It's not that I can't cry—my tear ducts work. It's that I don't like to. Because that makes me vulnerable. And I don't like to be vulnerable.

But I am, vulnerable—that is.

I'm one of the most sensitive, anxious, thin-skinned people you could ever meet. I have an extremely strong, fiery personality, sure and this paradox inside of me is part of what makes me interesting and fuels my high-energy temperament. (I've heard it called "ADHD," but I shirk labels.)

Here's another internal dichotomy that I've discovered it's time for me to embrace: I am weak, but my weakness is my strength.

My tender fragility is what makes me kind.

I know what it's like to be hurt, to be loved, to be cuddled—and to need all of these things in order to be a healthy person.

Because we all have qualities that we, or others, could perceive as weaknesses, when what they are in reality is our basic humanness that everyone possesses. Everyone.

We feel pain and we might cope and become hard and callous, but I truly believe that almost no one starts out this way.

We begin as tiny infants needing love and affection. Maybe we don't get it. Maybe we do. Regardless, we grow into adults, who are basically small children pretending to be anything else but that.

Here's what I think: it's when we get in touch with this vulnerability and learn to embrace and then express it, that this is when we're truly living life from an authentic place that's sadly often buried deeply within—and this expression out to others, in the forms of gentle words, soft smiles and honest conversations (and writing), is where we connect to others; really connect.

I don't connect to anyone, especially myself, when I embrace arrogance because my confidence took a fall. I don't connect either when I choose to harbor my emotions and hold them hostage, because I'm still feeling them, I'm just not owning them, and that's a lie.

Shedding tears on a consistent basis doesn't mean you're not living a lie, but trying to not make them happen does.

Still, the main issue that I had last night, besides missing the meeting and feeling quite a bit foolish, was that it made me realize that our new place isn't home yet.

Yes, we've moved around—and in every other place we inhabited, I told myself that it was temporary.

This one isn't.

We're setting down roots and forming a life, and not only for us, but for our daughter—and that's just it.

I can write and blog and think and live my life as a strong, independent woman, but the simple fact is that we do things for our kids.

Your life changes (or at least it should) when you bring a child into this world. There's a rawness that cuts through all the b.s. in life after you've seen that baby's newborn face. Being a parent forces you to embrace your weaknesses because they're right there in front of you, in the form of an extremely tiny human being.

So I might want my new part of Ohio to feel like home after a year, but it doesn't. I might still want it to feel like home in 30 years, and it still might not, but here's what I realized last night in my tearful frenzy— it's home to her, and that's all that matters to me right now.

To her, our new house is home, her school is her playground, she has friends who genuinely love and care for her, and this is her familiar comfy spot—and while I might never enjoy crying, I know that I'm a better mother, and a better woman, when I own every single part of me as special, as lovable, and as a strength.

Because the other thing is that I am strong, even when I cry. I'm also delicate. Here's what I'm not: breakable...and neither are you.

Your flaws, your less-than-ideal quirks—they make you who you are. Love them, embrace them, kiss them. If you don't, who will?

Sometimes we're all kids who get banged up playing a little too hard. That's life.

I guess, for the time being, I'll consider home to be the place where people are waiting for me to help make it better, to tell me that they love me exactly as I am, and to remind me that being vulnerable isn't always a bad thing—that learning to accept and desire all the facets of love, of life, and of ourselves, might just be the real gift after all.

"When we were children, we used to think that when we were grown-up we would no longer be vulnerable. But to grow up is to accept vulnerability…To be alive is to be vulnerable."

— Madeleine L'Engle

# Chapter 26

## Accepting Your Flaws

If you want to meet your higher self, then acknowledge your worst self first.

Here's the thing—owning your flaws doesn't mean that you're not on a path to self-betterment. In fact, I'd argue that you're farther along than most. Let me explain.

Do you have someone in your life about whom you could say that he or she will never change? Why?

Why won't they change?

Because they're ignorant.

If you want to let go of being an angry person, for example, then your first step is admitting that you have a temper.

If you want to eat healthier foods then you have to recognize that you eat crap.

And if you want to be a real yogi, then you have to want to change and grow and evolve. In short, you have to want to achieve yoga.

Do you know what yoga is?

Yoga is not a sweaty, 90-minute class that leaves your muscles hard and long.

Yoga is not reading as many books by Iyengar and Patanjali as you can.

Here's what it actually is: the cessation of the fluctuations of your mind. (You might find this especially interesting if you are reading Patanjali.)

Here's what that means:

You're present. (If you're driving your car, you're thinking about driving your car.)

You're also connected with the energy that permeates, that's always surrounding you—essentially, with the swirling chaos that is life—without ever letting go of the reality that there's a perpetually calm, serene, fluid energy that equally co-exists inside of you, underlying this changeability that encircles and, occasionally, that engulfs.

If you think that this sounds simple then you're either one of two things:

Naturally and deeply gifted with your yoga practice, or,

Not attempting to practice yoga.

My money's on the latter.

So what is a yogi (or yogini) for that matter?

A yogi isn't made because she's wearing Lululemon pants and has a monthly auto-renew pass at the yoga studio. She's made because she wants to achieve yoga, to become better, to grow and to evolve both spiritually and with how she's living and sharing her life.

That's why I consider myself a yogi.

Every single day I practice becoming a better person; someone who's honestly trying to make the world within which I live a more successful place.

Let me tell you, I've taken more steps backwards than I have forward.

I took a dozen steps back when I was slammed with post-traumatic stress. I was shoved backwards when my heart got broken. I was, thankfully, carried forward by a husband who loves me—and by my own will to bend not break.

And I know that I'm flawed, and imperfect. How does this make me anything besides what I am? (A mere mortal human being trying to walk the talk.)

If you think that yoga has to be one lifestyle with only a selection of choices (likely ones that you've read about rather than have experienced), then I feel sorry for you.

Those texts that you're reading and holding onto and those people that you're worshiping because of their wisdom and strength? They were written by people who walked through their own fire—who have done the work to get to that higher place that those of us on the yoga path want to also go—not by people who were afraid of getting burned.

So, yes, I am a yoga practitioner.

I'm also a drinker, a meat eater, a woman with an occasional potty mouth, and a hot head.

Here's a laundry list of some other things that I also consider myself to be: a mother with a giving heart, a person with an empathetic soul, an athlete, an early to bed and early to rise sort, as well as a yoga teacher and writer.

Was that last list a little prettier for you to read? Did it fit more within your framework of what you want me to look like?

Luckily, I don't care—I like me. I actually even like those other less-than-ideal personal attributes that I told you about too.

I remember when a close friend once told me a few extremely personal things about herself and she sadly thought that I wouldn't love her anymore after she bared these revelations to me, but do you know what she had really done?

She made it possible for me to love her.

Because love cannot exists unless you let me in.

Love cannot exist unless we're vulnerable in addition to being pliable.

Love can only exist when we love, and accept, ourselves enough to be open to potential rejection and pain, and doesn't this also relate to moving closer to your better self (towards "enlightenment" or the "yoga journey" if you like those terms instead)?

How can you grow if you don't first realize that you're a tiny seed with a shell to break through?

"Truth is by nature self-evident. As soon as you remove the cobwebs of ignorance that surround it, it shines clear."

— Mahatma Gandhi

# Chapter 27

## The Power in Only Having a Few Friends

Friendship is few and far between—and that's a good thing.

I've been to a rave only once in my life.

For those of you who aren't aware, a rave is "a large overnight dance party featuring techno music," according to Merriam-Webster, that is.

I have some colorful memories from this time, when a girlfriend and I went along with two other friends who frequented these late-night parties. However, even in my exuberant youth, I couldn't stay up late— and thankfully neither could she.

It was still the middle of the night, though, and one of the others had driven. In short, we were stranded and needed to find a way home.

We weren't desperate enough to wake up our parents, since it was still a ridiculous hour even though it was pathetically early to the other ravers.

I remember standing outside the club—and I use that term generously, as I'm pretty sure it was just an old warehouse in a gross part of Toledo, Ohio—with my buddy trying to figure out what to do.

Mind you, this was B.C. (Before cellphones.) I can still see her face contort with sorrow as she realized that we didn't really have anyone we wanted to call. She turned to me and said, "This is when you know that you don't have as many friends as you thought you did."

I remember another time in college, a few years after this above-mentioned scene, when yet another friend told me that her car had broken down at 3 a.m. the night before. She told me that when you think about who you can call at this unusual hour, you discover who your friends are. (Needless to say, she hadn't called me.)

As I grow older, I realize how much these lessons have taught me, even if much of it has remained in the deep recesses of my subconscious mind.

I'm a Scorpio. If you know absolutely nothing about astrology, I'll explain to you what I mean.

I have only a handful of close friends, although I socialize well and have many friendly acquaintances. Still, the point is that for these few people who I bring into my heart, and into the heart of my life, I would do just about anything.

I don't think there's anything wrong with owning up to the reality that most of us don't have 20 people you would call in the middle of the night for help. If you think about it another way, would you want 20 people calling you?

Friendship, real friendship, requires skill, work and dedication. It's simply not possible to give all of yourself to a billion people. I guess you could, but would you have any love left over for yourself afterwards?

I think my—I guess you could call it demanding—nature with friends most likely results from the fact that I'm an identical twin and am married to the man who has been my best friend since I was 14 years old. They both set the bar pretty high.

My twin sister taught me how to have a close relationship. Fortunately, I consider us both to be independent, so I don't feel that we learned co-dependency from our relationship either.

For me, it came naturally to fall into a long-term relationship with a boyfriend early on. I prefer genuine intimacy over b.s.-spewing conversations, and always have—and I think this helps explain how I feel about friendship as a whole.

Are you the sort of person who is different with different people or are you simply you, regardless of who you're with?

I consider myself to be "me," no matter who I'm talking to. I do know I had to work to be this way, because I think it's easy to default into people-pleasing and chameleon-changing when you're young and, quite frankly, still not entirely sure who this "me" even is.

It also seems to me that if you have a plethora of people you think are your friends, you might want to get yourself stuck in a bind and see who you turn to—and who answers.

Not everyone answers.

Not everyone picks up the phone for you in the middle of the night, ready to grab a coat and dash out the door even if you call expecting it.

Friendship is a two-way street, and this is the secret to any long-term or successful relationship: you must find other people who want these same things.

Not everyone is capable of being a good friend, and maybe not everyone wants to be a good friend.

My husband and sister still set my relationship bar high.

For lack of a better explanation, my back went out for the first time this weekend. My sister told me that she would figure out a way to come help with my daughter if I needed her. My husband did much of the work around our house and he played with our daughter so that I could do the only thing that makes me feel better—curl up on my back in a fetal position.

Having the inability to stand up straight and pick up your child makes you feel pretty vulnerable, let me tell you.

When you're vulnerable, who will you let in? (Because in serious pain, whether externally, like mine currently, or internally, as the case usually is, we don't have the strength to put up those phony walls for people who honestly are not our friends.)

Well, as it turns out, I do have a couple real friends. (Even though I recently told you about how lonely I've felt since my semi-recent move last year.)

Two of my (as it turns out, best) girlfriends are going to watch my little girl so that I can have a visit with my miracle worker, I mean massage therapist. They didn't even hesitate when I asked them for help.

Also, perhaps not ironically, I was just talking with one of these amazing women the other day, mentioning to her that I think for some of us the real difficulty lies in learning how to ask for and accept help rather than being overly dependent on others. (Although, this conversation came up in the first place because we were talking about people who had these tables turned.)

And that's another beautiful part about people—we're all different.

Finding people who are exactly like you is not how you find friends—but finding people who like you exactly as you are might be.

Relationships are odd things.

They require attention, but not so much attention that you suffocate them; they require love, but the necessary patience to get to know someone in order to arrive there; and they give more than they take, if you're really in a good one.

And I would rather have that handful of people who truly know me, love me, believe in me and support me through thick and thin than I would a mountain full of people who are none of these things to me.

Life isn't lonely at the top; it's lonely when you're in the middle of it, and of everyone, and you're still alone.

So I'm going to take a few minutes and send all my loving gratitude out to these beautiful people in my life. I'm especially thankful that my initial feeling of vulnerability led ultimately to an immense feeling of strength.

There is strength in love.

Here's another definition from Merriam-Webster for you: strength is "the quality or state of being strong: capacity for exertion or endurance."

That's another thing about love—it helps move us through life, and it helps us enjoy the process while we're at it.

"Being deeply loved by someone gives you strength, while loving someone deeply gives you courage."

— Lao Tzu

## Chapter 28

## Throw Away Your Bucket List

The sky is rumbling again.

Long, quaking echoes of thunder emerge from the storm that's beginning to water my garden.

My daughter and I are cozy inside, listening to Still Corners while she drives around her little Flintstones-esque car.

The earth is already saturated from last night's downpour, but not so much that it prevented us from heading out onto one of the park's gravel-lined trails for an early afternoon hike a few hours ago.

The crunch of the ground beneath my feet made my heart start to come alive the second that my shoes hit the stones.

The feel of sweat dripping inside of my tank top and catching on my upper lip instantly woke up my soul.

Exercise really does help me get rid of my monkey mind, of my perpetually moving brain.

I guess some people would call my mental style ADHD, and that's fine with me. I honestly don't mind labels—I just don't let myself be contained by them either.

I look up from where I sit typing now, with the rain and the music providing a steady, thumping backdrop, and I observe my little girl rolling around in her Cozy Coup, looking for the best way to get over the hurdle of gliding from the wood floor and onto the white-tiled hallway.

This morning I felt like garbage.

I woke up and my eyes were literally as red as my small lady's plastic car.

My typical morning coffee didn't do the trick, and neither did my bath.

Nothing, including getting out of the house for some crack-of-dawn errands, seemed to lighten my heavy spirits and awaken my downtrodden body—until I stole 30 minutes to work out.

My husband's a cyclist; he rides a single-speed up seriously steep hills, like the bad-ass athlete that he's always been, since well before I met him at age 14.

I slightly pathetically begged him to take our daughter for me while he finished up his own pre-work routine. (It wasn't yet 8 a.m.—I told you we've been lacking in the sleep department.)

I dashed downstairs to our workout area—free weights, an awesome Spinning bike that was my Valentine's Day present years ago (diamonds are over-rated) and my beloved Nordic Track, circa 1980-whatever.

Still wearing my dress, I tore off my short-sleeve cardigan and threw on my tennis shoes. I cranked up Incubus on my iPod (I admit to getting stuck on tunes from my youth; listening to the same album repeatedly for a week or a month before moving onto something else)—and I took off (well, kind of, I was stationary, I'm aware).

The music pounded and so did my beating heart.

I unwisely hadn't made as much time this past week to move my body as I normally do, having had several appointments and being hampered also by this recurrent soggy weather.

I watched the sky grow clearer through the large picture window in front of me as I rhythmically moved my feet along those stationary wooden skis— and I turned the music up louder.

I watched the clock, so as not to make my husband late. (He would almost assuredly rather slightly delay his departure than stop me from making myself feel better.)

The sky opened up and so did my mind—my own mental clutter and debris being swept away, my dress now sticky. (Don't worry; I changed.)

A little while later, after switching clothes, spending time with friends and having lunch, my little girl and I decided to get out onto our gorgeous local trails before the rain made its now familiar appearance once again (that crunchy hike on the gravelly trail I mentioned before).

She sang "Twinkle Twinkle Little Star" at the top of her lungs as I happily pushed her in her stroller, up and down the hilly terrain, listening to her perfectly pitched song and watching her cute hands move in motions that matched her words—and I got deliciously sweaty all over again.

I felt the pebble-littered trail beneath my rubber soles and heard the birds singing along with my tender child, as my thankful eyes drank in the lush greens and emotionally stabilizing tans and greys of the trees and rocks that surrounded me.

Later still, when the rain began to beat my windshield, I saw the steady motion of my wiper blades and listened all over again to my daughter's singing—this time a tricky medley of "Twinkle Twinkle" and the "Itsy Bitsy Spider"—and I can't help but wonder why we make things so hard on ourselves sometimes.

We watch our brains whirl and go and they don't seem to wait for us to catch up.

We get irritated with the other people that make up our world. (To be fair, some are more challenging than others.)

We don't pay full attention to what we're doing—and multi-tasking is a myth.

Yet often we don't have a choice—we have human responsibilities that get in the way of our more primitive needs.

I did it just this week by allowing my hurried schedule, and my subsequently tired but needy body, meander myself away from my usually disciplined workout routine.

And here's the thing—if we expend only a microscopic amount of additional time and energy paying attention to what our bodies are asking us to do (eat right, move around, and get some sleep for God's sake), then everything else becomes easier, naturally.

So while I won't pretend to know or even fully understand your own personal situation, I do have compassion. Because I, too, have a child who doesn't prefer to sleep as much as I (or not really much at all, if I'm being completely honest).

I also have a life that requires my attention, money and resources—usually outside from where I'd prefer these things to be—and that's life.

Life means having things to do that you wouldn't necessarily place first, but life should also mean making sure that you're fitting in some of that other good stuff along with it.

We don't need to be weekend warriors—what a waste of an opportunity if we save everything that we desperately want to do for a rainy day inside of a bucket list of dreams.

Do something every day that you would maybe only consider appropriate for a Friday night. Try it. Just once.

You might discover a different world—a better one—that's been waiting patiently for you all along, you've had only to notice it.

My daughter's singing trails off, and the rain is really coming down now.

I'm so glad that we went for that walk outside.

Not because I'm glad that I took advantage of the sunshine—although I am—but because now I can sit back and enjoy the cleansing sounds of the driving cloudburst, since I've already purified myself from the inside out—and I hope I'm teaching her to do the same.

I hope I'm showing my daughter that life isn't made of weekdays and weekends—it's made of opportunities that we take or let slip by. I hope I'm showing her, too, that inside of her human form lies an eternal well of energy, one that she can tap into at anytime, if she chooses.

Possibly I'll also help her understand that more often than not the solutions are right there in front of our faces, and that they aren't as complicated as we think they should be.

For me, my mental chatter needed a break, so I took my body for a walk. That's it. That's all I needed.

Life is difficult enough, and then we have to go and make it even harder.

I look back out my big front picture window and notice a clearing sky and patches of beaming sun and I'm grateful knowing that I'll sleep well tonight.

"If a man achieves victory over this body, who in the world can exercise power over him? He who rules himself rules over the whole world." — Vinoba Bhave

# Chapter 29

## Daydream Believer

I've always dreamed in black and white.

The times when my dreams have vividly been in color or when something within the dream is in color, like a brightly-tinted bridal bouquet in a Photoshopped wedding album, are moments that I cling to and remember.

We talk about our dreams.

We analyze them.

We might even pore over everything that we can in order to try making them come true—and there's a reason for that.

We hold our dreams near and dear to our hearts and, for me, the ones that I hold closest—the ones that I care for and nurture and water so that maybe someday they'll grow up to be big and strong—are my daydreams.

You know, those little, tiny seeds of infinite possibility that you don't even realize you're wanting or craving, or even needing until you snap back out of your waking vision, unable to ignore the longing that has finally been unlocked.

Admittedly, some of us daydream more than others.

Yet all of us have unaccounted ideas—things that we desperately want to see hop out of our childlike imaginations and onto the storybook pages of our real lives. So how do we get there?

How do we figure out what it is that we really want and then go after it once it's been discovered?

Now, I'm by no means an expert on how to be the perfect, dream-inducing individual, but I do know that I've let myself follow my own pathway to success, even when this has meant wandering away from the more practical course that I had originally set sail for. (And I've shared many of these meanderings with you).

So, from my daydreaming heart to yours, here are five steps that have, undoubtedly, helped me, and that I now hope will help you live up to your true potential.

Be grounded.

In order to realize your full potential, outside of your human requirements, you need to be able to live as a successfully grounded person first.

Dreams or no dreams, we live, hopefully, as people who are capable of having roots that grow into the earth because while we are dreaming, imaginative, wonderfully intangible beings, we are also animals that inhabit this plane of reality, and of daily living.

In order for a tree to grow toward the sky, possibly to ridiculous heights, then this tree has to be nurtured down here on earth, firmly planted in healthy soil.

Additionally and more importantly, if you find yourself always dreaming yet never making anything real, then your fantasies are of no good to anyone, namely not to you.

Get in touch with this more primitive side of yourself by exercising, eating well and placing much needed importance on other basics like shelter and work, so that your dreams have a foundation from which to grow and flourish.

(Re)Define success.

I told you earlier that I walked away from another, more practical, future. I left a college-fueled career to work in the typically less stable field of yoga teaching, and now I predominantly write—and this became easy for me to do when I redefined what success means.

To me, success means happiness—on an inner level that's challenging to verbalize—and I find that I'm, in fact, happiest when I'm helping other people and sharing my deep-seated passions. Aren't we all?

What are your passions? What makes you tick?

Personally, I want enough money to live and buy good food (see previous step), but money doesn't define my success. (Most writers aren't in it for the money—and the same can be said about most yoga teachers as well.)

If your success is defined more by money than mine, then this might be a limiting factor for you as to how far you're able to pursue some of your more wildly unrealistic goals (although, I do believe in return on investment). That's not for me to say, because my definition of success isn't yours, but you do need to figure out what yours is.

My suggestion is that if you're not satisfied with your current definition of success, that you strongly consider writing a new one. Don't worry, multiple drafts are more than acceptable, they're required.

The company you keep matters.

Oh, there are so many quotes, sayings and adages on the company that we keep—and the reason is simple and universal.

The people that you choose to spend your life with (and I'm not necessarily talking romantically) are important for two main reasons. One, they reflect who you see when you look into the mirror and, two, they help shape that reflection.

Choose people who support you, who support your definition of success, and better still, choose people who are adaptable enough that they'll encourage you while you're figuring out what your definition means, and, if necessary, they'll carry you and help you back up after you've fallen (because you will, if you're reaching high enough). Which leads me to...

Expect failure.

If you want to recreate your options and live up to your highest potential, then you have to expect to crash and burn, at least once and at least from time to time.

Being successful does not mean that you never fail. Rather, I'd argue that in order to be successful in any capacity and through any definition that you are by default welcoming failure.

There's a reason that there are a billion inspirational stories out there about people who fell—often many, many times—before doing something that the world never forgot.

"Failures are finger posts on the road to achievement." — C.S. Lewis

Be tenacious.

We all fail. All of us. It's how we deal with these failures, though, that matter.

(I'm thankful to my yoga practice—specifically my practice of balancing postures—for helping me learn how to get up more gracefully.)

On top of this, sometimes the road to success turns out to be entirely the wrong road, and it takes a lot of courage to turn around and start all over again.

If you search yourself and you find what it is that could make you happy—a new job, a move, whatever—then you are heading in the right direction, but you will have hurdles and setbacks—and if you don't have the confidence in yourself that you can overcome them, then who else will?

I'm a big believer in dreams.

I believe that all of us bring a quality of huge value into this world when we arrive, but I also know that life can be hard and frustrating, and that many of us lose sight of who we really are and of what it is that we really want while we're here.

I'm a writer and a yoga teacher, and yes, I have a degree in geology (that I don't regret). I'm also a mother, a wife, a daughter, a sister, a friend and a daydreamer—and you know what? The second that I've lost the last thing on this list, for me, the party's over.

Listen to what your heart is telling you.

Believe in yourself and believe in your dreams—
because you might just end up surprising yourself
when you try going after them.

"If your dreams do not scare you, they are not big
enough." — Ellen Johnson Sirleaf

# Chapter 30

## Twenty Life Truths for Everyone

There are many truths about life.

One is that life isn't fair; another is that you don't want to sit downwind of your lactose intolerant friend after she just ate cheese—and here are a few more:

1. No one trusts a gossip.

2. Numbers on the scale only mean so much.

3. It's unnecessary to wash your hair every day.

4. But it's okay if you do.

5. Facebook friends who constantly share workout advice in the vein of P90X and how many squats they did before breakfast are annoying.

6. If you're still talking about it, then you haven't "let it go."

7. Women like sex too.

8. Lying only works for so long.

9. Everyone needs help.

10. Money really doesn't buy happiness.

11. But having enough doesn't hurt either.

12. Laughing makes you feel better.

13. Vagina isn't a bad word.

14. Asshole is.

15. Great love takes work.

16. We all have time to exercise.

17. Perfection isn't attractive; your wonderful, little quirks are.

18. We should speak the truth, with love.

19. Thoughts become words and actions, so hone your thoughts into the words and actions that you want to live.

20. Live each day like it's your first, not your last.

"Truth is like the sun. You can shut it out for a time, but it ain't goin' away." — Elvis Presley

# Chapter 31

## Own Your Inner Bitch

There's a falsehood that repeatedly circulates and that fallacy is that people (be it man or woman) don't like aggressive women—and I wholeheartedly disagree.

And it's not about being a tactful bitch or even a pretty, smiley one—no, it's more direct than that. Here, without mincing words, is how to be a strong, independent, go-getter that others will still want to be around.

Like yourself.

The way that we treat people comes from within. When we like who we are and accept everything about ourselves—like our aggressive nature, if we have one—then we're so much more likely to accept others for who they are—and it shows.

Don't fight.

Yoga practitioners strive to reign in their churning, swirling thoughts by training the mind to be still—but this is not the same as fighting who you truly are. Some of us are born easy-going, for instance, and some are not. (I can especially vouch for this as a loving mother.) It's imperative that we own up to our more innate qualities so that we can fully develop them and then let them shine.

We are not gods.

Yes, you can be an aggressive individual who has the confidence to assert yourself easily, but please remember that your way isn't the only way or always the best way either.

Again, as a mama, my daughter is much less obvious than I am in the way that she shares her opinions and thoughts, but just because she's a tad quieter and calmer about her delivery doesn't mean that I shouldn't pause and appreciate her perspective.

In short, yes, be your aggressive self, but let's not forget that we are not better simply because we're louder.

Be strong enough to back off.

It takes a lot of personal discovery and, often, experience to learn when a situation calls for boldness and when the boldest action is silence and patience. Continue searching and practicing.

Be kind.

An aggressive person is still a kind one. Self-confidence is easily mistaken for self-centeredness, although these two don't have to go hand in hand.

Part of the reason for this faulty bias is that emphatic, self-confident people are not afraid to be big and bold and shiny—and this can be intimidating. Consider that it's not our job to make others feel comfortable with our own radiance, but, equally, that we can be empathetic and understanding.

Own it.

I've been writing a book on being a recovered anorexic and a huge part of anorexia is trying to make yourself smaller—and I don't mean physically. Everyone is done a disservice when we try to cram our vibrancy into tiny packages to make others more comfortable with our presence.

The root of it all.

Get in touch with the why of your fearlessness, because it's when we act out strongly from a place of fear, intimidation and, basically, ego that we are not being strong—we're being jerks.

Don't live your life to be liked.

The bottom line is that some people will like you while others do not. Living our lives from a place of neediness is not only unhealthy but unattractive. Be okay with who you are—and be okay with less than perfect appraisals.

The deceptive story that aggressive women are bitches in a negative sense only borders on true when that aggression comes from a personal belief of self-deficiency and a reaction of bullying; driven by a demand to justify and prove our worth.

However, when we connect with our biggest, brightest inner selves and then shine out to the world from this place of love, we're radiating love and light—and, well, what's not to like?

"Our deepest fear is not that we are inadequate. Our deepest fear is that we are powerful beyond measure. It is our light, not our darkness that most frightens us. We ask ourselves, 'Who am I to be brilliant, gorgeous, talented, fabulous?' Actually, who are you not to be? You are a child of God. Your playing small does not serve the world. There is nothing enlightened about shrinking so that other people won't feel insecure around you. We are all meant to shine, as children do. We were born to make manifest the glory of God that is within us. It's not just in some of us; it's in everyone. And as we let our own light shine, we unconsciously give other people permission to do the same. As we are liberated from our own fear, our presence automatically liberates others."
— Marianne Williamson

# Chapter 32

## What Your Happiest Self Wants

Yesterday I was such a grump. I told my husband that my body felt like dog poo.

All week long my yoga practice had been ho-hum, my runs were inconsistent, and I was feeling just plain yucky.

This morning, however, I decided that it was high time to turn my mood around—so I took my tiny lady and her jogging stroller out for a run on my favorite trail.

The sunshine peeked through the trees, not quite sure if it was ready to be awake yet. (I can relate.)

The grass and foliage were lush and green thanks to all the rain we've had here in Ohio.

My body moved, and as it did the tightness drained, not only from my muscles, but from my mind and heart as well.

Aaaah, this is life.

Way too often I get caught up in the cerebral part of being human and forget to just move and breathe and be an animal.

Which led me to ponder those days that start out great (like today) and are wonderfully serene and happy throughout, right up until my head hits my pillow.

What is it about these days that make them so fantastic and joyful?

So I came up with this list of things to do if you want to enjoy simply being alive.

Move your body.

Do something that gives your body a little bit of exercise every single day. You don't have to hit the gym or go to the yoga studio or even dedicate a full hour—just do something, anything really.
A few of my preferred mood-boosting body moves are: dancing in the kitchen with my daughter while making dinner, taking a short walk in nature and breaking out five minutes worth of yoga core moves in the middle of the day (talk about quick energy).

Drink water.

As you know by now, I love water—obsessively and adoringly. I know that some people find water to be a boring drink, but your body needs it, so drink up anyway.

Laugh.

Find small ways to add laughter into your day.

Whether you call a friend who always cracks you up or you watch a hilarious SNL skit you love on YouTube, it doesn't matter. Better still, lighten up in general, and notice the humor that exists in your every, ordinary day that you often completely ignore. (If you're really at a loss then watch a child—they find delight in those little, tiny moments that we adults sadly stopped noticing years ago.)

Be authentic.

There's nothing unhappier than being phony. Try as hard as you can to let down your guard and just be the real you regardless of your setting. Easier said than done, I know, but it's well worth the effort because putting on different masks for different people is exhausting. Consider being open to the possibility that you are wonderful exactly as you are.

Eat healthy food.

Ugh, eating crappy, processed food is sure to make your entire system feel lousy.
Fill up every day on fresh fruits and vegetables—and pay attention to how good it makes you feel.

Yet still allow treats.

I absolutely believe in eating dark chocolate and drinking wine and hoppy beer—in moderation.

One of my favorite ways to complete a good day is to break out one of my teensy, pretty chocolate plates along with a couple squares of the good stuff.

Do your chores.

I sincerely do not like housework. I don't like doing the dishes. I have a severe disdain for laundry. And you know what? Too bad. I have to do it anyway—and I always feel better after I do.

Reach out and touch someone.

People are made to connect. We need affection and good ol' fashioned touching. Spend time cuddling with someone special and I promise you'll feel amazing afterwards.

Remember tomorrow.

When I felt horrible yesterday, I knew that I would feel better today. Sometimes the best thing you can do for yourself when you're feeling down or things aren't going exactly as you'd like is to remember that, thankfully, life is an ever moving ocean filled with changing tides.

Practice kindness.

I'm telling you this from personal experience—being a jerk will not make you feel good. So, smile and extend your kindest you out into the world—because it's entirely true that the love you take is equal to the love you make.

I think I'll stop here, because the thing about happiness is that it's not complex.

Happiness is noticing and then hanging onto those little things in life—hugs, sunshine on your skin, the after-effects of a great workout—that we too easily let slip past us.

"Happiness is not something ready made. It comes from your own actions." —Dalai Lama

# Chapter 33
## Life Is Not a To-Do List.

Saturday rolls around and it's easy to get caught up in the mental scan of household chores and family needs.

But it's important to consider that weekends are for more than grocery store trips and lawn care.

I remember waking up as a kid on Saturday morning and being allowed to spend these early day hours in favorite, cozy pajamas watching my favorite shows. It was special.

I'm sure my parents cut the grass, weeded the garden and cleaned the house, but that's not what stuck with me.

What stuck with me was the family hikes on local trails, playing in the backyard and family meals, which is exactly why even as an adult I'm careful to not let my brain become overloaded with what my adult self wants to accomplish come the two adjoining days that many of us have off.

And life is not a to-do list.

We're so willing to check things off an imaginary societal list of ordinary accomplishments.

Graduate high school, check.

Go to college, check.

Move out on your own for the first time, check.

Graduate college (many years after you initially started), check.

Get married...have kids...blah, blah, blah.

And when someone doesn't coincide with these essentially made-up expectations, we question their societal worth and placement or encourage them strongly to fit back into line; to keep checking off this list.

Yet here's my thought on this particular Sunday morning, where I sit typing at my nicked, antique wooden table, with my daughter and her favorite cartoon in the background and my husband on a mountain bike ride:

What if we threw away our to-do lists?

What if we pretended that each day was something to just be in awe of?

What would happen if every morning became a fresh start towards who we want to be and a new beginning of potentially the best day of our lives?

And, yes, we'll weed the gardens and mow the lawns. We'll clean the dust off our bookshelves too. But we'll also not pretend that this is what life is about, because it's not.

They say that people on their deathbeds rarely wish they'd worked more or accomplished that one nagging task. Instead, they wish they'd spent more time with their children or opened sheltered hearts to love with more willingness.

But life is hard.

It's filled with things that need to get done and sometimes, unexpectedly, shit happens. At the same time, though, we possess the internal ability to simply shift perspective and, often, it's this little, teensy tiny inner transition that makes huge life changes.

I wake up and yawn and stretch through my toes and roll over to my side. I grab my glasses lying nearby and wait until my daughter wakes up so that I can see her sparkly eyes and good-morning smile. And while I know that our day will have errands and things that I need to do, I don't focus all of my energy this way. Instead, I borrow her wonder-filled, childlike mindset that enables her to see these everyday routines as fun and part of something much larger and not, incorrectly, a mundane reality.

I hate doing the dishes.

Yet when I ask my daughter to help me with them, every single time I'm rinsing off the last wine glass and singing one final round of "The Wheels on the Bus" and wondering how it all got done so quickly.

And, no, I'm not suggesting that we ignore our chores or even our societal checklists (I'm glad, for example, that I got married and had kids). But I'm not going to pretend that all I want out of my life is a clean house and short grass.

Maybe that's why we have the prevalent midlife-crisis syndrome.

We spend so much of our lives climbing monetary ladders and putting checks next to arbitrary accomplishments that we forget to listen to beating hearts and to feed the fires that ultimately fuel us for longevity.

So, today, I'm checking "love passionately" off of my to-do list. Yep, done.

I'm also putting an imaginary mark next to "watch favorite cartoons."

And as I prepare to more officially begin my Sunday morning, I'm walking into the next several hours with an open heart and mind, and maybe, just maybe, I'll even have some fun doing the laundry (if it gets done, that is).

# Chapter 34

## One Breath at a Time

I was in yoga class this morning, thoroughly ecstatic to be there.

Driving there, I was at a light that just turned green, facing a pick-up truck.

We were both kind of in the intersection doing nothing until he turned on his turn signal. I was initially annoyed at this disregard of his signal, until I quickly shoved down my own left blinker to signal my own turn, mine also, apparently, disregarded.

Embarrassment crept into my heart as I told myself that it was early and I was not yet awake, but this rising pink color of my cheeks was more from my quick readiness to not extend this other driver the same courteous break.

And then I was in class, with my mat down and my blocks set just so and my towel placed just there, when a stranger placed her mat unnecessarily close to mine and then her block unnecessarily close to my mat and then her folded jacket behind my mat rather than hers.

Annoyance rose within me once more.

I took a yogic breath—a pause—and quietly—silently—reminded myself of my already similar morning lesson.

Yes there are cubbies for jackets, but wasn't my blue jacket also folded and placed behind my mat on this particular day too? Maybe she wanted hers nearby for a particular reason, like I did.

And so what if her mat was closer than it needed to be.

All week I'd been experiencing loneliness, so I asked myself if she had been my sister next to me, for instance, wouldn't it be true that she could place her coat where she wanted and her sticky mat nearly on top of mine without either bothering me in the slightest?

What if she were the friend that I'd been wishing I had all week long.

And my week-long lesson—my continual, current moment of progress and my seemingly lifelong regression—is realizing that my judgment often stems directly from a lack of both patience and knowledge.

Knowledge comes to us along with wisdom and time, and when I'm quick to throw around an unnecessary assessment, it's generally because I don't have enough information at hand to offer the situation something much more wise, something much more valuable, than my opinion: empathy and gentle kindness.

It feels awful to be judged.

It feels terrible to know that someone is picking us apart and dissecting us with their nonchalant—and completely unimportant—conclusions.

I distinctly remember walking on the towpath one breezy, tropically lush morning with my daughter, pushing her stroller, when I received a phone call that I had to take.

This happened well over a year and a half ago and I can still see the contorted face of the unknown man on a bike as he turned around to throw me his disdainfully judgmental face after he'd ridden around me; he having no idea why I was on my phone and that, normally, I didn't even pay attention to it when walking in nature (probably, generally, like him).

And this unbridled impatience that leads to snap perceptions is the exact same thing that I do with myself.

My lack of patience towards my flaws and challenges and, equally, towards myself in relationships with others leads to my own improper self-rating. This is why we often say that people who judge others most harshly are often judging themselves the worst.

Yet the inverse of this sorry equation is also true.

I slow down—I take a deep yogic breath—and my ability to open my eyes and heart to a more sincere truth becomes available because I've slowed down and can take much more in.

And wisdom and its sister compassion arrive when we slow down, breathe and are receptive to a story in its entirety—and let's be honest that we usually never have a story in full.

We witness tiny parts; we are given access to an infinitesimal piece of another's personality or situation and, frankly, who in the hell are we to judge anyone, especially given this simple, ignorant reality?

So as I inhale and momentarily still and close my eyes, and as I exhale and feel my fingertips prance across my laptop keyboard, I invite within my life and within myself this gift of patience that I might slow down and practice being with each moment as they occur for me and for those around me, rather than haphazardly brushing off unseen intelligence as incorrectly unimportant.

I invite into my heart space this appeal to slow down and take it all in, one breath at a time.

# Chapter 35

## How to Walk Clear-Eyed and Barefoot Toward Unknown and Unwanted Change

Her heart feels strangely set free.

She's struggled and moped and hobbled her way through these last few weeks, only to come out on the other side a little bit stronger and a lot more resilient.

Yet, isn't that how life often goes?

We face challenges and are presented with uncomfortable circumstances, which we can either wade our way through, only to bloom like the lotus from its home of murky waters, or we stay stagnant or, worse, drown. But, more often than not, we grow and blossom and reach back up towards the sun with our shade-tired, sunlight-thirsty petals—after a descent period of darkness, overgrowth and, sometimes, sorrow.

Because moving forward and into new territory isn't easy, but here's a secret: Life isn't meant to stand still, and the people who come out on top—happy, content and fulfilled—are the ones who stay curious and ready for change.

It's true that movement brings turmoil.

The windy spring weather can conjure sweet, breezy gusts that ruffle a slightly warmed face and tickle the hearts we wear on our sleeves, but winds can also be too strong—they can make us feel fragile and insignificantly mobile as life blows us around and around in an unsympathetic whirlwind.

And we can hold on for dear life—we can grope and cling to the sides of something slippery and not meant for stability—or we can let the winds blow us past the metaphorical fork in the road.

This doesn't mean, however, that we always seek the new—the different—experience.

Generally speaking, the grass typically isn't greener and those who flit and float from space to space are usually trying to leave themselves behind (which is, fortunately and unfortunately, impossible). But those of us who like routines and are comforted by earthy steadfastness can find life's frequently mutable transitions more than unsettling—we can find them downright disturbing, tiresome and depressing.

Here's the thing, though: We have no choice.

Life will, inevitably, present us with opportunities to grow and widen in who we are, and it's when we stand tall in our previously created roots and let ourselves be open to embracing this unknown that we are finally able to move into who we truly are and who we have the ability to be.

Because we create our own boxes.

We put ourselves in our own confines of labels, and can and can't-do's—and, in truth, we are so much more than a simple definition of success or failure.

We can be ready to fly—but still accepting of a meager takeoff.

We can process who we know we have been while still leaving our boundaries smudged just enough to expand beyond them.

We can be anyone we want to be, but what we want can be limiting—if we don't want to move from the cozy bed that we've already created, and slept in night after night.

It's hard getting out of bed some mornings, isn't it?

I want to stay buried underneath sheets, with my body warm and my nose slightly cold. I want to flip my pillow over for one more round of the cool side. I want to begin a new day, but I don't always want that beginning to come as quickly or unexpectedly (those nights where sleep feels like it lasted for five seconds rather than seven hours).

But it's here—and hanging out underneath the sheets won't change that.

So I get up.

I make myself a coffee and I get excited about a new morning filled with everything that I've never experienced before.

This brand new second is a complete revelation in my life, and so is this one and, while they might not be what I was looking for or waiting for, they're here to seize, and one thing I've learned is that it's actually much safer to grasp onto life in this manner than it is to cling to the irrational, precarious walls of what we wish could stay the same.

And here's another thing I've learned: When life presents us with the same experiences, circumstances or set of problems more than once, the universe is slapping us in the face with our own denial; saying, "This is something to open your eyes to."

So, today, I open my eyes to what lies ahead—even if right now my road is currently obscured by (unexpectedly gorgeous) wildflowers.

And I open my eyes to my deepest, clearest truth— that I am more than capable of moving into the unfamiliar.

After all, familiarity and comfort only arrive with enough exposure—and I'm finally not afraid to lift my veil and walk barefoot past that fork in the road, towards my destiny.

# Epilogue

We are not our human limitations.

We are not an arbitrarily contrived, societally perceived, measurable scale of success and failure.

We are more.

We are not our seemingly cement-filled shoulders.

We are not our aching back.

We are not our ability to walk.

We are not our reading capability.

We are not our ability to speak.

We are not our intelligence.

We are not our bad knee.

We are not our worn joints.

We are not our scoliosis.

We are not our heart conditions.

We are not our handwriting.

We are not our surgery scars.

We are not our emotional wounds.

We are not our cancer.

We are not our golf score.

We are not our epilepsy.

We are not our eating disorder.

We are not our body image.

We are not our ability to fit our beautiful bodies into an unimportant size.

We are not our parental style.

We are not our anxiety.

We are not our anger issues.

We are not our depression.

We are not the amount of money we own.

We are not our student loans.

We are not our job title.

We are not our skin color.

We are not our glasses.

We are not our relationship status.

We are not our hair.

We are not the clothes we wear.

We are not our hearing aids.

We are not our athletic performance.

We are not our genetic disorder.

We are not our chronic pain.

We are not our Interstitial Cystitis.

We are not our mood swings.

We are not our ADHD.

We are not our autism.

We are not our learning abilities.

We are not our sleep disorder.

We are not our diabetes.

We are not our asthma.

We are not the medication we take.

We are not the car we drive.

We are not an arbitrarily contrived, societally perceived, measurable scale of success and failure.

Whether or not we see ourselves and our abilities positively or negatively, we are not our low self-esteem or our ego.

This doesn't make our human limitations problematic—they are a part of our experience and something to be recognized, owned and honored.

But we are more.

Today, and every day, let's celebrate being more.

# Write Your Own Happiness

My husband and I were driving down a hilly, country road near our house the other day when we observed a strangely clad woman walking up her driveway, away from her mailbox.

She was wearing a blue ankle-length skirt adorned with white flowers, along with a slightly flowy yet structured white blouse—and big duck boots at least a few sizes too large.

My husband noted her oddly original outfit selection, while I looked at the clock on the dash of our VW Jetta and offered, "No, she's a teacher who just got home and wanted to check her mail, so she put on the nearest thing to the door, her husband's boots."

My own husband then quickly glanced over at me, interested but surprised, from behind the steering wheel and said, "That's why you're a writer. You saw her, and you could create a story like that, and it fits."

"Hmm, well, I think that's the truth. I think that's what happened," I replied. "Maybe I'm a writer because I'm observant. I notice things."

Why do you write or better yet, why do you read?

I know that I have a decomposition book filled with pages and pages of these "nothing" sorts of observations, those little things that my brain wants to try to recreate into words from where they sit, deeply lodged inside of my mind after a touching experience.

Like the way I feel summer dawning when I watch the sticky watermelon juice dribble down my deliriously happy toddler's chin as she stuffs as many of the little, pink chunks of fruit into her mouth as she can handle, simply to see her tiny cheeks puff up like a chipmunk in the "mirror" of our oven door.

Or how I can't stop listening to The Jesus and Mary Chain album, Stoned & Dethroned, and that this instantly transports me back to teenage memories, fueled by young love that became long-lasting and hormone-raging arguments that only seemed to solder those two youthful hearts together, after those angsty emotions had zoomed by.

Still, sometimes I don't write when I probably should.

I have a finished memoir that I spent a good year and a half trying to find an agent for. I sincerely believe that it's beautiful, and that there's a place for it on our collective literary bookshelf, but at the same time, I haven't even started to write that other book—the one that's long been brewing around in my head, well before I ever contemplated beginning this completed one—and why or, better yet, why not?

Possibly, when we love to read—and I mean love to read—we doubt our own ability to write.

After all, who can write another *War and Peace*, or even another *The Giving Tree?*

Regardless, it seems that for as long as people could make and share stories, they have. Some are better than others, some are truly great, and a few are masterpieces that we never forget. Yet the one thread that weaves through basically all of these tales, connecting even the most unexpected, is the subject of happiness, or the loss of it.

Lately, I've come across a lot of articles and blogs on ways to achieve happiness. Come to think about it, I've actually written a good-sized handful of similar material myself.

We're always searching for happiness—looking so hard that we pursue even the pursuit of happiness.

What is happiness, anyways?

I won't pretend to be able to summarize that answer for everyone but for me, happiness looks like a few things.

It looks like:

1. Coffee combined with morning light so new that you think you're the only one awake anywhere, while you're four-fifths of the way through your favorite novel (the one that you never want to finish, but have to finish because you can't wait to get to the end—you know, that moment in that novel forever, with your coffee and sunrise).

2. Bread rising in the oven, that I see through the slightly dirty glass door, accompanied by that particularly nutty, mouthwatering aroma that I know people for centuries have also smelled.

3. Half-empty wine glasses sitting around a scratched-up antique table in front of your favorite people, who can't help but be slightly slumped back in their chairs from eating your deliciously home-cooked meal.

4. The peak of the summit of your favorite mountain trail coming just into view at sunset, right before you set up camp with your favorite person next to you.

5. My daughter's face on the pillow next to me in the moonlight before I fall asleep, where I can just make out the curve of her soft, pillowy lips in the blue-black of the room.

Happiness looks like a lot of other things to me too.

I think that's why I write—because I am happy.

Even when I'm writing about pain, there's something sweet nestled inside; a small, intangible seed of knowledge that something beautiful will indeed rise from these ashes of my horrors.

I have a blue phoenix tattooed on my right arm.

I drew it meticulously, over and over again on torn-out lined notebook paper during fifth period study hall of my senior year in high school. It represents to me now exactly what it did to me then—that there is no death.

There is no lifeless, angry fire.

There's only the soft, brilliantly rising re-birth that continually touches our fate, from our reality on a basic, cellular level to my own belief that there has to be more than this—more than me sitting on my red sofa typing my seemingly arbitrary thoughts, hoping you'll read them and find at least a little bit of something worthwhile buried within.

I guess that possibly I'm a writer because I see meaningful stories in deceptively simple places—or maybe, just maybe, I'm offering to you that life is what we make of it.

When it seems that life isn't what you want—when you find yourself reading about happiness, yet unable to catch it—remember that somewhere inside of you happiness already exists—you have only to acknowledge it, to witness it, and to claim it.

We write our own stories.

"Either write something worth reading or do something worth writing." — Benjamin Franklin

The next few pages are your turn to begin writing your own happiness. Take a few minutes each day to reflect on each quote, and then dive into exploring it on your own.

Enjoy!

"Your pain is the breaking of the shell that encloses your understanding. It is the bitter potion by which the physician within you heals your sick self, so therefore, trust the physician and drink his remedy in silence and tranquility." — Kahlil Gibran

"To be idle requires a strong sense of personal identity." — Robert Louis Stevenson

"My potential is more than can be expressed within the bounds of my race or ethnic identity." — Arthur Ashe

"I don't want to be perfect, but I do want to be a role model. My mom always tells me that imperfections equal beauty. All of us are imperfect." — Miley Cyrus

"I've never been a conceited person or cocky, never felt boastful, but I always had a sense of self-worth; I always had a real sense of myself." — Will Ferrell

"It is not in the stars to hold our destiny but in ourselves." — William Shakespeare

"Girls see these defined roles they're supposed to follow in life, but when I was a young child, my parents told me I could be anything." — Joan Jett

"Our stories come from our lives and from the playwright's pen, the mind of the actor, the roles we create, the artistry of life itself and the quest for peace." — Maya Angelou

"The high destiny of the individual is to serve rather than to rule." — Albert Einstein

"If I were to tell you that your life is already perfect, whole, and complete just as it is, you would think I was crazy. Nobody believes his or her life is perfect. And yet there is something within each of us that basically knows we are boundless, limitless."

— Joko Beck

"One must still have chaos in oneself to be able to give birth to a dancing star." — Friedrich Nietzsche

"Promise me you'll always remember: You're braver than you believe, and stronger than you seem, and smarter than you think." — A.A. Milne

"Love isn't finding a perfect person. It's seeing an imperfect person perfectly." — Sam Keen

"Beauty is truth's smile when she beholds her own face in a perfect mirror." — Rabindranath Tagore

"The universe is not required to be in perfect harmony with human ambition." — Carl Sagan

"Tell me I'm clever, Tell me I'm kind, Tell me I'm talented, Tell me I'm cute, Tell me I'm sensitive, Graceful and wise, Tell me I'm perfect—but tell me the truth." — Shel Silverstein

"If the world were perfect, it wouldn't be."

— Yogi Berra

"If you hear that someone is speaking ill of you, instead of trying to defend yourself you should say: 'He obviously does not know me very well, since there are so many other faults he could have mentioned.' "

— Epictetus

"Master your instrument, Master the music, and then forget all that...and just play."   — Charlie Parker

# Acknowledgements

There is no way to fully thank everyone who has inspired me to live my best life. However, I'd like to thank a few people by name.

Kate Bartolotta, thank you for being my vigilant supporter, fabulous and hard-working editor and, mostly, for being my friend and reminding me of the love that exists between soul sisters. This book wouldn't exist without you, and not entirely because of your labor, but because of your constant belief in my work.

Thank you to everyone who has helped me on my journey as a writer. Thank you, Michael Miller, Jason Wachob, my college professor Dr. Troutner, my supportive elementary school teacher Mrs. Stowe (who told me even then that I would surely grow up to be a writer), Brianna Bemel, Bryonie Wise, Sara Crolick, and the influential Waylon Lewis (and to everyone at elephant journal, an elephant trunk nuzzle).

Thank you, Mom, for buying me blank books to write in and for telling me that my first story (and every one after) was a masterpiece. Thank you for your friendship and for teaching me the meaning of unconditional love.

Thank you, Dad, for listening to me and encouraging my ideas from as early as I can remember (which is pretty darn early). Thank you for treating me both as a bright, independent spark and your little girl.

Thank you to my twin sister, Sarah, who is clearly my loudest cheerleader, my confidant, the moon to my sun, and the only person on earth who completely gets my zany sense of humor. (i carry your heart; i carry it in mine.)

Thank you, Todd, my husband and partner since the tender, angsty age of 14. This book comes out the day before we celebrate 20 years together. I can't possibly articulate our years of adventure, passion and friendship, nor can I describe the wondrous light that you bring into my life simply by being you.

Thank you to my daughter Gemma. I can't fathom teaching you a fraction of what you've already taught me. You are a blazing spirit who lights up the entire world. You ignite my heart and you bring out more stories than I could ever write down. I credit you fully for my prolific writing and, equally, for reminding me that stories are only as good as the life being lived outside of them.

And thanks to you, the one holding this in your hands and reading, if you've made it this far, my inappropriately short list of names.

Thank you for wanting to share in what sets my soul on fire and for wanting to explore with me how we can create together a world filled with love, authenticity and joy.

"Don't ask what the world needs. Ask what makes you come alive, and go do it. Because what the world needs is people who have come alive." —Howard Thurman

Jennifer S. White is a voracious reader, obsessive writer, passionate yoga instructor, drinker of hoppy ales, and devoted mama and wife (a stay-at-home yogi). She considers herself to be one of the funniest people that ever lived and she's also an identical twin. In addition to her work on elephant journal and Be You Media Group, Jennifer has over 40 articles published on the wellness website MindBodyGreen and her yoga-themed column *Your Personal Yogi* ran in the newspaper Toledo Free Press. She holds a Bachelor's degree in geology, absolutely no degrees in anything related to literature, and she currently owns a wheel of cheese. If you want to learn more about Jennifer then make sure to check out her writing, as she's finally put her tendencies to over-think and over-share to good use.

Made in the USA
Lexington, KY
16 August 2014